Why theory?

MANCHESTER
1824

Manchester University Press

Why theory?

Cultural critique in film
and television

Edward Tomarken

Manchester University Press

Copyright © Edward Tomarken 2017

The right of Edward Tomarken to be identified as the author of this work has been asserted by him in accordance with the Copyright, Designs and Patents Act 1988.

Published by Manchester University Press
Altrincham Street, Manchester M1 7JA
www.manchesteruniversitypress.co.uk

British Library Cataloguing-in-Publication Data
A catalogue record for this book is available from the British Library

ISBN 978 1 7849 9310 8 hardback
ISBN 978 1 7849 9311 5 paperback

First published 2017

The publisher has no responsibility for the persistence or accuracy of URLs for any external or third-party internet websites referred to in this book, and does not guarantee that any content on such websites is, or will remain, accurate or appropriate.

Typeset by Out of House Publishing Ltd
Printed in Great Britain
by CPI Group (UK) Ltd, Croydon, CR0 4YY

In memory of Ralph Cohen, 1917–2016,

the father of literary theory

For Annette, my beloved wife for fifty years

Contents

Acknowledgements

I wish to thank most warmly the friends and relatives who have helped by suggesting films and television programmes for use in the text: Emma, Beau, and Jamie Grimes for *Spanglish*, *The Help*, *Spider-Man*, and *Iron Man*; Sue and Peter Tann for *Breaking Bad* and Kelli Rudolph and Dunstan Lowe for *Weeds*. The title, *Why Theory?*, comes from Sasson Pearl, a good friend for many decades, who asked this question in response to a careful reading of the first book on this topic, *Filmspeak*. I am also grateful to Dr Ana de Medeiros, who kindly invited me to lecture on the book to her students at the University of Kent Centre in Paris and suggested the present publisher. Commissioning editor Matthew Frost of Manchester University Press responded positively to the plan for the book and steered the manuscript masterfully through the procedures of acceptance, evaluation, and revision. The finished typescript was then placed in the care of the assistant editor, Paul Clarke. Rebecca Willford and Liz Hudson meticulously copy-edited the final version. The reader for the press, Aaron Jackson, provided valuable comments for revision: I thank him for his careful reading and constructive criticism. My greatest debt, as with all of my previous publications, is to my wife, Annette Tomarken, my most rigorous critic and best editor/proofreader.

Films and television programmes cited

Chapter 1
Quartet (2012)
The Best Exotic Marigold Hotel (2011)
Salmon Fishing in the Yemen (2011)
Spider-Man 2 (2004)
Iron Man 2 and *Iron Man 3* (2010, 2013)

Chapter 2
Mr Holmes (2015)
The West Wing, series 1, episode 1 (1999)
The Second Best Exotic Marigold Hotel (2015)
House of Cards, series 1, episode 1 (2013)
Frozen (2013)
The Railway Man (2013)

Chapter 3
Mad Men, series 6, episode 1 (2013)
Spooks, series 10, episode 3 (2011)
The Iron Lady (2011)
Spanglish (2004)
Philomena (2013)
The Hundred-Foot Journey (2014)

Chapter 4
The Butler (2013)
Belle (2013)

12 Years a Slave (2013)
Django Unchained (2012)
Breaking Bad, series 1, episode 1 (2008)
Sherlock, series 2, episode 1 (2012)

Chapter 5

The Invisible Woman (2013)
Magic in the Moonlight (2014)
Lincoln (2012)
Homeland, series 1, episode 1 (2011)
Mr Turner (2014)
Peaky Blinders, series 1, episode 1 (2013)

Chapter 6

My Week with Marilyn (2011)
Downton Abbey, series 6, episode 5 (2015)
The Artist (2011)
Boardwalk Empire, series 1, episode 1 (2010)
The Help (2011)
Weeds, season 6, episode 3 (2010)

Introduction

The idea of using films to elucidate literary theories came from my classroom experience of teaching undergraduates the fundamentals of literary theory. Students who had great trouble with the arcane language of theorists were able to grasp the ideas by way of films, a medium that for them was less off-putting since most theorists are writing for other specialists, not undergraduates. I began to search for films that illustrated the ideas presented in the classroom, and the students helped guide me to movies they liked and understood but that also had relevance to the course. Undoubtedly I learned as much if not more from them about film than I taught them about theory. *Filmspeak* was the result of that experiment: the volume analyses six theorists who represent, in my view, the fundamentals of literary theory, providing the foundation for those who came after them. The present volume uses a similar format. Each chapter contains three key ideas, and each of these three sections uses two examples of films or television programmes to exemplify the concepts. My hope is that the general reader will be familiar with many of these mainstream movies and television programmes.

The initiators of literary theory in *Filmspeak* were, for the most part, writing in the 1950s, 1960s, and 1970s, when literary theory was first recognised as a separate discipline, that is, when postgraduate students could for the first time specialise in – or at least list as a field of interest – literary theory. So the premise of this book, like that of the previous one, is that literary theory is a new critical genre that arose in the middle of the twentieth century for reasons to be discussed shortly. Here it is important to point out that there are alternative conceptions of literary theory, the most prominent being that it is a development of philosophy, specifically, a recent form of aesthetics. By contrast, I follow in the footsteps of my teachers, Ralph Cohen and Northrop Frye, who believed, first, that theory was the handmaiden of practical criticism, arising as a result of problems confronted in analysing specific works of art, and, second, that in attempting to resolve those problems theory moved to a higher level of generality than that of practical criticism. As Cohen suggested in his formulation of literary theory as a genre, this new genre, like all other genres, is a part of a larger system, be that literary criticism, aesthetics, or any other branch of knowledge. The point of describing theory as a genre gives new emphasis to the specifics of literary theory. In other words, to employ like Cohen the image formulated by Hans Robert Jauss, literary theory has an orbit of its own although within the solar system, itself a part of the cosmos. The separate orbit of theory makes possible the study of its development in relation to itself, that is, in terms of previous theorists and other disciplines, from literary criticism and aesthetics to philosophy and history (Cohen, *Future* 55). My task in this book is to elucidate a part of that orbit, to reformulate its place within broader disciplines without precluding or replacing the encompassing or cosmological procedure that is the object of all forms of the humanities.

Before considering the rise of literary theory, let me make clear that I am not a specialist in film and therefore cannot use the technical language of film experts. The movies in this book serve as illustrations of the ideas even though it is hoped that the procedure is reciprocal, that the films shed light on the ideas as well the reverse. Also, the films chosen are mainline features directed towards a large and varied audience; that the films appeal to a general viewer is essential because an important part of my argument, to be pursued later in this introduction, is that these ideas have filtered down or up, as the case may be, into our culture. This infiltration of our culture occurs not because movie producers and directors are interested in theory – I am sure they are not – or because theorists have a special relationship with films – I am sure they would agree with me that they do not. Rather, these ideas have become a part of the *Zeitgeist*, the spirit of the age, the world view, whatever term is selected to refer to the climate of thought characteristic of an era or a culture.

Considering literary theory as a separate discipline distinguishes my work from similar books in the field. For instance, Mary M. Litch and Amy Karofsky's *Philosophy through Film* (London and New York: Routledge, 2002) uses film to elucidate certain issues in philosophy, such as 'Truth', 'Scepticism', and 'The Problem of Evil'. The present study is not concerned with philosophy or these sorts of problems except in so far as they bear upon literary and art criticism. Even on the odd occasions in this volume when philosophical issues do arise, my assumption is that such questions change structure in an artistic context, leading often to different kinds of resolutions than are found in studies of philosophy. At the same time, I do not intend to compare theory and film, crossing disciplines, as in the interrelations, say, between architecture and music or literature and painting. Natalie Melas, in *All the Difference in the World: Postcoloniality and the Ends of Comparison* (Palo Alto, Calif.: Stanford University Press, 2007) warns of the dangers of such comparisons based, as she points out, on nineteenth-century universalist assumptions about human nature that are no longer generally accepted. I agree with her wariness of such an assumption: 'We exist, we think, we write in the presence of all the cultures in the world without possessing them in any single concept or idea' (Melas, xii). No attempt is made to cross the boundaries of cultures or disciplines; certainly my lack of expertise on film would prevent my moving into that medium, and cultural comparisons are left to experts like the anthropologist Clifford Geertz and the sociologist Pierre Bourdieu. The relationship between film and theory in this volume is explanatory, avoiding on the one hand philosophy through film and, on the other hand, a comparison of film and theory as disciplines.

My view of literary theory as a new discipline, instead of suggesting parallels to other disciplines, sets it apart, emphasising among other distinctions the fact that it only began in the mid-twentieth century. At the time of its inception, various kinds of formalism dominated the critical scene: structuralism in Europe, Leavisite textual analysis in Great Britain, and New Criticism in the United States. Essentially, these doctrines derive from the Russian formalists writing at the beginning of the twentieth century who asserted that the structure or form of a work of art points to immanent themes. The clearest formulation of this notion is contained in Austin Warren and René Wellek's *Theory of Literature* (1949). The theory of norms advanced in this book argues, as Ralph Cohen pointed out, that a work of art functions like a layer cake: any way you cut it, you cannot avoid the layers or norms, that is, the central themes. Literary theorists called this notion into question, pointing out that the discovery of these themes was a function not merely of the work of art but also of the responder, the reader, the audience, you and I, what T. S. Eliot called the 'hypocrite lecteur', who respond on the basis of cultural beliefs and predispositions – the term used at the time was 'ideology', one that I try to avoid because it is more ordered and coherent than our basic assumptions. These early theorists asserted that belief systems changed in history and varied with different societies.

At present, various cultures surround us. At the same time we are threatened within and without by terrorists trying to destroy our society. Cultural theory addresses these problems. For this reason I call this book *Why Theory?*, echoing a question put to me by one of my wisest friends upon receipt of my previous book. In *Filmspeak*, I focused on trying to make accessible to a wider audience theorists who used a specialised and arcane language. As I came to the end of that volume a paradox became apparent. While questioning the implicit cultural assumptions of formalists, these theorists were themselves partaking in a shared, if erudite language – and one of the most important innovations of structuralism is that language is culture – of their own. And my attempt at translating that language into common parlance involved at least one foot inside that door of exclusion and privilege, provoking my friend's question, Why theory? In short, literary theory seems to be practised by a small number of academics; why should the general public want to understand it or be a part of that cerebral club? This book is an attempt to answer that question by suggesting that theory can help us understand cultures, our own and others. Specifically, cultural theory provides a means of comparing and distinguishing cultures instead of merely dwelling in our own limited environment, helping us come to terms with how other cultures are changing us from within and threatening us from without. Before spelling out that idea I have to admit to a great embarrassment. While I argue that theory from 1970 to 2000 took for the most part the form of cultural theory, that stage has now passed. Few present-day literary theorists equate their project with cultural critique. A study of the new perspectives of the most recent period, from 2000 onwards, will be my next project. For our current purposes, where literary theory is going is less important than the present direction of our culture(s): literary theory of that earlier period speaks to this issue.

The next logical question after 'Why theory?' might be 'Why film and theory?' I discovered in the classroom not only that the students were more at ease with visual than written media but that the arcane ideas of literary theory are insinuating themselves into popular art: since most of the films in this volume derive from printed narratives and other genres, popular media in general can be said to be the source of these ideas. However, films designed for a general audience have the widest appeal and serve as examples to a broad, perhaps the broadest, audience. And since, as I have already pointed out, the producers and directors of movies are not theorists and may know little about it, the ideas come from the culture, the mental climate of the time. One of the implications of these cultural ideas, at first glance seemingly the esoteric concern of academia, being present in this popular art form relates to our preoccupation with the problems caused by the clash of cultures; this issue is not merely a matter of concern to theorists but to all thoughtful people of our time.

Film criticism, however, is abundant, ranging from newspaper reviews, recommending what to see or to avoid, to journals specialising in film theory. My aim, however, is neither to judge the films nor consider them in relation to film theory. I shall try to interpret them in relation to ideas derived from literary theory. The first step towards steering a middle course between movie reviews and film theory is to insist on what Geertz, examined in Chapter 1, calls 'thick description', a form of analysis that he associates with literary criticism. And here begins the most powerful argument for the relation between the social sciences and literary analysis that led to the era of cultural criticism. A recent news story provides a vivid example of Geertz's concept of thick description. A young woman in Pakistan recently survived by a miraculous accident a family 'honour killing'. Refusing to accept the spouse chosen by her uncle and father, she married the man of her choice. Eventually finding her among the in-laws, her father and uncle asked to take her back, solemnly promising not to harm her. When back home, she was severely beaten by the uncle and father who then shot her and threw what they assumed was her dead body into a river. Somehow she survived and courageously decided to pursue a legal case against her family, a rarity because few survive and among those who do the fear of reprisals usually prevents any legal action. However, this woman won her case in court. Yet the uncle and father received no punishment. Why? Because in Pakistan there is a law permitting the victims and their families to forgive the perpetrators of 'honour kill-ings', and there is immense social pressure on families, particularly in poor areas where most of these crimes occur, to forgive the crim-inals because these people with such meagre resources are heav-ily dependent upon one another. Pressing charges and demanding punishment lead to continued alienation between families that can result in harm and even death to other family members simply from the resulting estrangement from friends and neighbours.

It is readily apparent to many of these people that 'honour killing' is a 'primitive' custom that has no place in the modern world and that those who practise it must recognise that it is no longer appro-priate, if it ever was. We have been hearing and saying this for years but little has changed. The thick description above, however, reveals something new, namely, that the basis of 'honour killing' is poverty. Even families who do not agree with 'honour killing' and/or are the victims of it are likely to permit it to continue, not because they believe it to be right but for the survival of the family, especially for the victims, who fear that pursuing legal restitution may produce reprisals against the rest of the family. A thick description – and, of course, it is no accident that it is a description of a story, perhaps the most basic literary genre – pushes further into the texture of the spe-cific context than the familiar truisms or what Geertz calls the laws of social science. Geertz's notion of a thick description applied to culture is vividly depicted in *Spider-Man 2*, particularly in reference to his definition of culture as a web that we spin and within which we live. A thin description of Spider-Man would emphasise how he swings freely among the skyscrapers of New York City, transcend-ing the world, swooping swiftly above those below immobilised by traffic jams. A thick description would note that he is ultimately constricted by his own web, whose boundaries are set by the sky-scrapers, the hallmark of New York City.

Like the Spider-Man movie, the Pakistani story may be no more than a story. We respond to the narrative relying on the BBC World Service for the accuracy of the facts, taking us to the realm of the historian. Hayden White, in Chapter 2, confronts this dilemma. White admits that the historian is constricted by the facts whereas the literary storyteller is free to wander in the world of fiction or to mix fact and fancy. At the same time, he also asserts that the facts alone are not enough. The historian tells a story, lest he put us to sleep with a mere chronicle, a series of facts, what Benedetto Croce describes as 'one damned thing after another' (189). The ability of a great historian to weave the facts into a tapestry that is vivid, interesting, and informative is essential to history. For White, that ability is derived from art as understood by critics analysing how and why art succeeds in interesting and teaching us. For him, history is not a science but an art that makes use of scientific means of research, that is, attempts objectively to sort out the facts. However, once the historian moves beyond the research stage to writing up his findings, he crosses over into the literary realm, at least in part, in order to tell a coherent and compelling story. White therefore argues that history at its best never arrives at the 'last word' on a topic; on the contrary, the facts can always be rewoven into a different story, which is what actually happens in history. The history of history, how stories are revised in different ages, is to some extent a function of different needs for different cultures, accommodating changes within cultures. White believes that the way we form our historical narratives is a function of our culture(s) and that meta-history, the study of the changes to the bases of history, of its methodologies, is also intimately bound up with cultural history. White concludes, as does Geertz, that the narrative element of their respective disciplines requires the art of literary interpretation and that it is in this overlapping of disciplines that theory serves an important role, a notion that is now widely accepted but in the 1970s was considered controversial. White's conception of the intermingling of fact and fiction is aptly illustrated by the opening episode of *House of Cards*, where we see a modern version of *Macbeth*, a completely fictionalised tale of Washington ambition that we nonetheless believe to be possible, even probable, and thus representative of a truth about the heart of government in the United States.

A theory of interpretation is also important for Julia Kristeva in Chapter 3. Since interpretation gives equal weight to subject and object, the question for Kristeva is 'What about female interpretation?' She describes three stages of feminism. The first is a kind of militant separatism that, once it has established itself and been widely accepted as a necessary and valuable innovation, moves on to a middle stage. Now the feminist is reintegrated into the male-dominated society and it is acceptable to be a mother, but a separate female language is cultivated to avoid total domination by the male culture. In the final and last stage, which Kristeva admits is only an ideal and far from reality, the male/female difference is internalised in what she calls the nucleus of both male and female beings. In this final stage or phase, as Kristeva calls it, the female interpretation has equal status with that of the male, not standing against it but accepted side by side with it, within the psyche of the enlightened person, male or female. However ideal, the point is that once interpretation is seen as an essential element of our knowledge, then different viewpoints must not only be tolerated but also accommodated within the dominant perspective. Nonetheless, that does not mean for Kristeva that even at that ideal stage sexual difference vanishes. Rather, the war between the sexes evolves into a kind of dialectic, opposites interconnected in a field where their power and influence are equal. This position is illustrated at the end of *Philomena* when Martin and Philomena confront the nun who has lied to both Philomena and to her son, even as he was dying of AIDS. Martin's response is to suggest that if Christ were present he would have tipped the nun out of her wheelchair. Philomena, on the other hand, refuses to be angry and forgives her. In my discussion of this film I shall suggest how these two contrasting views come together for Martin and Philomena but in very different ways.

Difference that remains after the truce ending the war between the sexes is also what Homi K. Bhabha has in mind with regard to the perspective of the subaltern and, by extension, that of all oppressed people. 'Hybridity' is the term Bhabha applies to the psyche after colonialism, and to other situations. It refers to both the dominant and the dominated because, as in Hegel, the master–slave relation always involves both, never one without the other. But Bhabha insists, against Hegel, that this dialectic does not develop or lead to transcendence to a higher state. The wound of colonialism leaves a permanent scar on both ruler and ruled. Bhabha's careful analysis of the psychological aspect of colonialism leads him to a 'thick description' of the oppressed personality – and the oppressor is always also oppressed – that resembles the literary interpretation of character. Bhabha's work, while admittedly much indebted to literary analysis, also derives from his personal experience of colonialism. Born and educated in India, Bhabha went to Oxford for his advanced degrees; he now occupies a named chair at Harvard University. However abstract his formulations, Bhabha's experience of colonised and coloniser is vividly personal. He insists that analysis, whether literary or from any other angle, does not alleviate the

situation, however much it may clarify and render it more compre-
hensible. Bhabha implies that some deep parts of himself formed
during his early years in India are fundamental to his theory and
to his very being. In the film *12 Years a Slave* we see this principle
vividly exemplified at the end when Northrup, freed from his twelve-
year ordeal as a slave, enters his original New York home and when
greeting his family behaves as if he were still a house slave.

Pierre Bourdieu, the subject of Chapter 5, calls this element of
our personality the *habitus*. Bringing a sociological sensibility to
the discussion, Bourdieu argues that our habitus is formed early
in our childhood, involving basic tastes in food, furnishings, and
colour preferences that are determined by our surroundings and
upbringing. Habitus does not lead to complete determinism; it sets
certain ultimate parameters, but within those limits personal choice
and individual difference are permitted. The other factor that for
Bourdieu needs to be taken into account is what he calls 'field', as
in fields of endeavour, such as medicine or law, but also referring to
the context of our daily existence. Habitus in a field, for Bourdieu,
leads to a 'lifestyle' with the proviso – and here he approaches the
literary notion of character – that similar habitus and fields can
lead to very different lifestyles. Bourdieu's system of habitus–field–
lifestyle is a means of suggesting how we can maintain our belief in
our freedom of individual development but recognise nonetheless
that we are contained within our culture; we may indeed choose,
but the choices available to us are provided by our culture. Most
literary critics of the last three decades of the twentieth century,
trained in the concept of considering the context of character, feel
at home with this notion. Bourdieu's principles are clearly seen in
Lincoln where the habitus, 'honest Abe', as he was then called, sub-
jected to the field of Washington politics during the last few months
of the Civil War, chooses the lifestyle of the emancipator of slaves
rather than either ending the war sooner or attempting to establish
complete equality for black people. This choice enables Lincoln to
satisfy his conscience within the limitations posed by the American
political climate of the 1860s. By the end of the twentieth century –
I shall touch on this matter in the conclusion – questions arise about
how much freedom Bourdieu's system permits, or, in theoretical
terms, how much he allows for the full expression of individuality. At this stage, he provides a means of placing the relatively free
individual within his or her culture. Eventually, it became apparent

that the ultimate limits of culture present serious ethical problems. What, for example, are we to make of newcomers to the west who wish to live by and apply sharia law?

This kind of ethical question is pursued by Martha Nussbaum, whose position is discussed in Chapter 6. I conclude with her work because she is in one sense with the other theorists in the volume but at the same time points ahead to the next stage, one beyond cultural critique. Nussbaum's great innovation is what she calls 'love's knowledge'. She pursues an alternative to the two prevalent philosophical positions on ethics, those of Immanuel Kant and Jeremy Bentham. Kant believed in the principles of moral duty, something he assumed was available to all intellectually competent adults. Compromising these principles because of special circumstances is for Kant a form of condescension because the nature of duty is clear and not subject to dispute. Bentham, on the other hand, argued with equal absolutism for utilitarianism, for principles of right versus wrong based not upon duty but upon what most advances a particular goal. Nussbaum suggests an alternative that is more literary in nature. When reading a novel we must, according to Nussbaum, begin with empathy for the character(s) in the situation and give proper attention to that context: then and only then are we in a position to judge the character(s) from an ethical perspective. The love that Nussbaum has in mind is empathic contextual understanding, what we do every day when we listen to a friend speaking to us about what is troubling them. As a loyal friend, we make every effort to understand their point of view and the situation that engendered their problem. The television series *Weeds* provides an example of Nussbaum's ethics. As a mother, Nancy Botwin always loves and protects her children, even when one commits murder. One episode makes understandable to us how, in violation of moral duty and utilitarian goals, she can understand why her son committed murder and aid his flight from justice without our losing respect for her as a mother. When presented in an art form that evokes our empathy, love's knowledge is seen as part of the natural instinct of a good mother.

Interestingly, Nussbaum, writing in 1989, is disappointed that since adopting the ways of literary criticism she finds little interest in ethics on the part of critics. But ethics presents a very difficult problem for the cultural critic. We may empathise with the person brought up under sharia law who wishes to continue to abide by it in a nation that does not recognise its validity. We cannot let the matter rest there. The case of 'honour killing' mentioned earlier is perhaps an extreme example, but ethics sometimes forces us to make choices between cultures, something that is not available to cultural criticism. In this respect, Nussbaum points to the next stage of theory, after 2000, and it is for this reason that she represents an appropriate conclusion, her position evidencing an understanding of the cultural critics but pointing beyond them.

My conclusion develops the notion that although we may not believe our daily concerns are related to literary theory, we live surrounded by the questions and problems raised and discussed by the theorists analysed in this volume. The clash of cultures both within our own culture and from others without requires the kind of 'thick' analysis pursued by the theorists included in this volume. In their struggles may lie the answer to the question 'Why theory?'

1 Clifford Geertz: thick description

I begin this study with the work of Clifford Geertz because he articulates what he calls the 'interpretive turn' in his field of anthropology from science to the humanities, in particular to the mode of textual analysis used in literary criticism. Geertz emphasises that in his discipline science provides a thin description using rules and laws that explain little about the specific situation. For a 'thick description' Geertz turns to literary-critical practice. These two terms, the interpretive turn and thick description, will be key throughout this study. Geertz points to three aspects of culture that would profit from the thick description of literary analysis: serious game theory, sidewalk drama, and behavioural text. Each of these topics is the subject of a section of this chapter. With regard to serious game theory I analyse Quartet *and* The Best Exotic Marigold Hotel. *The next section, on sidewalk drama, looks at* Salmon Fishing in the Yemen *and* Spider-Man 2. *In the final section, on behavioural text, my focal points are* Iron Man 2 *and* Iron Man 3. *The central thesis of this book is that the phase of literary theory that emphasised cultural critique was the direct result of the interpretive turn to thick description.*

In the period from 1970 to 2000, the focus of much literary theory turned to the realm of cultural studies. I begin my study of this shift with Clifford Geertz, Professor at the Princeton University Advanced Institute from 1970 until his death in 2006, because he explains with admirable clarity that cultural studies needs to adopt the methods of literary criticism: 'Believing with Max Weber, that man is an animal suspended in webs of significance he himself has spun, I take culture to be those webs, and the analysis of it to be therefore not an experimental science in search of law but an interpretive one in search of meaning' (Richter, 1368). Geertz uses two phrases that will be important for this study, the 'interpretive turn' and 'thick description'. The 'interpretive turn' refers to the move in cultural studies from a social science seeking laws to a humanistic project with the aim of interpretation. The second phrase, 'thick description', makes clear that the kind of interpretation Geertz has in mind resembles that pursued by the literary critic. An article in *The Observer* on 11 May 2014 entitled, 'After the Crash We Need a Revolution in the Way We Teach Economics' may help explain the difference between thin and thick description. The subtitle provides further clarification: 'Students who claim that economics courses fail to explain the 2008 crash are gaining support from British business. Here, two Cambridge academics, Ha-loon Chang and Jonathan Aldred, say it's time for a change'. The article goes on to explain that Chang and Aldred believe that the problem with the present method of teaching economics is that it resorts to laws that apply to everything and therefore explain nothing.

> The most important thing about mainstream economics today – and a source of pride among many of its supporters – is that it is not limited to the study of anything in particular. It is defined by its tools of analysis (mathematical models mostly) rather than the object of inquiry. This is why so many recent popular economics books have claimed to be about 'everything' (15).

Clearly, students of economics are frustrated by 'thin' omniscient descriptions that offer no help in understanding a specific crisis. And yet it seems very likely that when these students graduate they will be confronted in a job interview with the question of how they would avoid a crash like that of 2008.

The Observer is suggesting that economics, like Geertz's discipline of anthropology, may have to give up its claim to being a social science and turn to the methods of humanistic interpretation to explain particular but crucial problems like the banking crisis of 2008. Thickness is Geertz's way of locating the kind of depth of texture that is the mark of literary commentary; avoiding reduction of the text, the literary critic endeavours to do justice to the work of art in concrete and detailed terms with little interest in placing the art object within some larger category, such as a law or abstract principle. In the past, Geertz admits, social scientists have been wary of literary interpretation because it seems subjective, simple assertions of opinions without evidence. Geertz believes that the best evidence for an interpretation is the specifics of the cultural situation, which entails treating that situation in the way a literary critic approaches a text, pointing to the language and structure as evidence for an interpretation.

In fact, Geertz asserts that the turn to the humanities, or what he calls 'the interpretive turn', represents a major change in how we think about how we think. The opening chapter of possibly his most famous book, *Local Knowledge*, is entitled 'Blurred Genres: The Refiguration of Social Thought', and the use of the literary term 'genre' is no accident. Here, Geertz advances three main ideas towards the goal of 'thick description':

> The recourse to the humanities for explanatory analogies in the social sciences is at once evidence of the destabilization of genres and of the rise of 'the interpretive turn' and their most visible outcome is a revised style of discourse in social studies. The instruments of reasoning are changing and society is less and less represented as an elaborate machine or a quasi-organism and more as a serious game, a sidewalk drama, or a behavioral text (23).

These last three phrases provide focal points for Geertz's argument that anthropology is turning away from objective science and towards humanistic interpretation. Accordingly, serious game theory, drama analysis, and behavioural text will serve as the topics of the three sections of this chapter. Each of these phrases will be explained at the beginning of the section devoted to it.

Serious games: Dustin Hoffman's *Quartet* (2012) and John Madden's *The Best Exotic Marigold Hotel* (2011)

Game theory, Geertz explains, involves serious games, that is, not just playfulness for amusement but also contexts for competition with rules and regulations in schools, workplaces, and on social occasions. Of course sports are where most of us first confront games and their rules, and sports commentary is, we tend to forget, often very 'thick' in Geertz's sense, so involved in the specifics that those who do not understand or follow the sport may be as puzzled as general readers are by specialised literary analysis. And that is Geertz's point: analysis of games, be they sports or serious games, must imitate the literary critic and become immersed in the specifics in order to offer an interpretation or explanation of victory or defeat. Serious game theory, according to Geertz, derives from three main sources:

> Wittgenstein's conception of forms of life as language games, ... 'following a rule' ... Huizinga's ludic view of culture, ... play as the paradigm form of collective life ... and von Neumann's and Morgenstern's ... [notion] of social behavior as a reciprocative maneuvering toward distributive payoffs (24).

Geertz emphasises the elements common to all three:

> What connects them all is that humans are less driven by forces than submissive to rules, that the rules are such as to suggest strategies, the strategies are such as to inspire actions, and the actions are such as to be self-rewarding – *pour le sport*. As literal games – baseball, or poker, or Parcheesi – create little universes of meaning, in which some things can be done and some cannot (you can't castle in dominoes) so too do the analogical ones of worship, government, or sexual courtship (you can't mutiny in a bank) (25).

Language is here the key factor: from the referee's or umpire's decision to the interoffice memo, the world of games, from playful to serious, is subject to rules communicated by way of language (both body and verbal) that has its own rules. For Geertz, the goal of this new method of social game analysis is to understand other cultures while maintaining the integrity of our own. He insists that we need to understand the games of other cultures, for in that way we enter the fabric of a way of life different from our own. I think of Robin Williams describing cricket as baseball on Librium.

> The primary quest for any cultural institution anywhere, now that nobody is leaving anyone else alone and isn't ever going to, is not whether everything is going to come seamlessly together or whether contrariwise, we are going to persist sequestered in our separate prejudices. It is whether human beings are going to continue to be able, in Java or Connecticut, through law, anthropology or anything else, to imagine principled lives they can practicably lead (Geertz 234).

Serious games in Quartet

The serious game in *Quartet* is the 'restaging' of the vocal quartet from *Rigoletto* for the purpose of raising enough money at the yearly Verdi Gala to support the retirement home where all the characters in the film reside. The selection from the opera and most of the other musical pieces are actually performed by professional singers and musicians while, for the most part, the actors and actresses mime their parts. In this sense, the audience plays its part in the game, a sort of cinema opera game, although the 'principled purpose', by which Geertz means something more serious than mere personal diversion, is not the same for us as for the residents/actors. The game for the audience becomes most overt at the end of the film when we see that in fact almost all of the actors are at or near retirement age. The credits show what the actors and actresses – now well beyond their prime – did in their heyday, at the high points in their careers. Seasoned performers, we are reminded, have just finished playing and playing at being seasoned performers. The serious purpose of the game for us is to show how these accomplished performers cope with ageing, playing histrionic games, competing with and joshing one another like members of a large family. In short, there is a certain element of reality in their being at Beecham House, a retirement home. That the game they play is a serious one is most poignantly clear for Billy Connolly who announced recently that he has been diagnosed with Parkinson's disease. Yet he continues to struggle on with his earthy sense of humour, punctuated in the movie by moments of vertigo, and in his daily life by the challenges of his illness.

The central game of the film, however, is confronted with a problem, a real problem. Two members of the quartet who were once married are now estranged, barely on speaking terms. After great effort on the part of the other residents, these two agree to sing together again, which in turn results in their being reconciled as a couple. The games in this film are multilevelled, and each level has a different aim while contributing to the larger goal. On one level, the actors rehearse the scene from *Rigoletto* to save their retirement home. The game here is not only that the performance is mimed but also that the performers, now elderly, cannot be expected to perform up to their old standards. On another level, they re-produce the quartet that brings the estranged lovers back together again, serving another goal than their immediate one, knowing, as Wilf (Billy

Connolly) points out, that Reg (Tom Courtney) and Jean (Maggie Smith) are still in love with one another. On still another level, we see and hear a sort of opera or musical comedy about the trials of old age, the interpersonal relations of public performers who must learn to live together in a community founded – rather embarrassingly, as Jean points out – on charity. Our interest is aroused by the fascinating acting of those playing the part of gaming, or playing at acting – Maggie Smith and Tom Courtney are particularly brilliant – and how successful they are at convincing us that ultimately for them, that is, for the characters they portray, the game is real. In the end it matters less whether or not we believe that Reg and Jean are in love than that they can pull it off as actors in a sort of comic opera/fantasy, a marriage proposal delivered and accepted while entering the stage for a performance. After all, it will be, if it is to be, a marriage of consummate actors, another performance. The ultimate reality here is that of actors ageing with grace and vertigo, competitive humour and companionable affection.

As veteran actors and singers they make the games more overt than the reality. In fact, they occasionally need to be reminded of the reality that is not theatrical. For example, when Jean (Maggie Smith) initially refuses to take part in the quartet, Cissy (Pauline Collins) brings her flowers in an attempt to convince her to participate. Losing her temper, Jean throws the flowers at poor Cissy, who reverts temporarily to a childlike state of senility. Later Jean apologises, realising that her 'hard to get' attitude had serious consequences, but she redeems herself later when Cissy, immediately prior to the performance of the quartet, reverts again to senility, believing she must return home to her parents. Instead of contradicting Cissy as the others try in vain to do, Jean humours her, leading the way to pack their bags, mentioning unobtrusively that the trip is to take place in a few weeks, thereby providing time for the performance, rather than directly contradicting Cissy.

Quartet is a film about the game or games of a retirement community, a group of people trying to keep their minds and bodies active by doing what they like doing or once did. For those who enjoy the film – and judging from my friends not all do – we enter a community of old actors and actresses who are brilliant at playing what they in fact are: oldsters struggling with old age. Perhaps the game here, the acting of ourselves, provides a perspective encouraging humour about ourselves that helps us be more companionable to one another. In any event, the games here all have cultural significance. And Reg, in his opera classes for local young students, is able with tact and delicate self-deprecation to discover how to relate rap to opera. Cleverly, he encourages a young would-be rapper to perform a sort of rap opera that establishes rapport (to be a bit punny) between Reg and the young people, and we next see a number of them in the audience at the opera. The rap opera could be described from the point of view of those familiar with pop rather than classical music as a thick description of opera. Moreover, the relationship between these two musical genres leads to a mutually informative conversation between Reg and the rapper and between the young students and the retirees. In Geertz's terms, the genres of classical opera and rap singing have become blurred, suggesting not just a mixing but also a mutual understanding between two different cultures. The marriages, however, at the end of the film between Jean and Reg and between rap and opera leave us wondering if this conclusion is merely a histrionic gesture, something great actors can bring off on screen but that is not likely to happen in reality. Geertz, of course, has in mind the world beyond the walls of the movie theatre.

Serious games in The Best Exotic Marigold Hotel

The Best Exotic Marigold Hotel makes very clear that the differences between individuals are but microcosms of the differences between cultures. The cultural element of the game is much more prominent in this film since the main cast of British actors is, after a brief introduction, transported to a retirement hotel in India. The contrast between the two cultures is made manifest by the fact that Sonny (Dev Patel), the manager, has misrepresented his hotel as a paradise for retirees when it is in fact struggling financially and dilapidated. The games involve each individual with their specific needs and desires coping with and learning to adapt to the rules of Indian culture. Muriel (Maggie Smith) gradually comes to tolerate, even enjoy living among people of colour whom she had previously regarded as her inferiors; Evelyn (Judi Dench), a widowed housewife, discovers how to use her communication skills and express her affection; Graham (Tom Wilkinson), a retired High Court judge, comes to terms with his homosexuality.

The principled or serious – Geertz uses the terms interchangeably – results of these games are comically surprising. Having experience looking after household expenses, Muriel believes she knows how to make the hotel a going concern: discovering a new tolerance, even affection for the 'natives', she decides to take up permanent residence in India. Evelyn helps train local telephonists and begins a new love relationship. Graham makes peace with the man he loved in his youth who he finds, to his delight, has not been ostracised for his homosexuality. The merging of the cultures of east and west is by no means one-sided. Sonny, for example, refuses to marry a partner to be chosen by his mother and eventually convinces her to accept his 'modern' girlfriend as his wife. Indeed, each of the characters gradually learns how to combine or reconcile elements of both cultures, the most prominent example being the arranged marriage of Graham's lover enabling him, unlike the British judge, to enjoy a respectable marriage with a woman.

Each relationship in the film suggests different ways in which the two cultures clash, merge, and lead to new kinds of interrelations. To begin with the most negative, Jean (Penelope Wilton) remains in her room, alienated by all that is different, allowing her husband Douglas (Bill Nighy) to experience the new culture on his own. In fact, Jean is more attracted to the High Court judge Graham (Tom Wilkinson) than to her husband but is humiliated when he admits to being gay. Of all the characters, Jean is the only one who ends up alone, estranged from her husband, a sad but predictable resolution for someone who has refused to open herself to the 'foreign' culture of India, vividly manifest in her insisting on giving orders to the hotel staff in a raised, exasperated voice. Douglas, like all the other guests at the hotel, goes out into the new culture, discovers new beauties and horrors and begins a relationship with Evelyn (Judi Dench). What attracts him to Evelyn is her interest in Indian culture. She teaches the young women at the call centre how to speak on the telephone to British retirees like herself and in turn learns about young Indian women. She bargains with local merchants and, after at first being taken advantage of, develops into a good businesswoman. Even here the results are two-sided; she must learn to haggle but also makes friends with the merchants. Similarly, Muriel (Maggie Smith) in spite of her prejudices begins to become attached to one of the maids at the hotel and to Dev (Sonny Kapoor) struggling to keep the hotel afloat. Graham also ventures out beyond the hotel looking for the Indian man he loved in his youth. The result here is also reciprocal. Graham is relieved that his youthful liaison had not ruined the young man, but he also realises that his Indian friend leads a freer and happier lifestyle than he ever experienced in his prestigious position in England. Even the cynical Madge (Celia Imrie), who seems to care about little else but finding a rich husband or lover, ventures into the new culture, unleashing her insatiable desires on Indian men. Whether or not that is good for Indian men is a matter of debate, but it does represent for Madge a move beyond the colour line.

The cultural interchange is also seen from the Indian perspective. Sunaina (Tina Desai) violates the sexual mores of her culture out of love for Dev. Not surprisingly, Dev's mother (Lillette Dubey) forbids her son to marry Sunaina. Then Young Wasim (Honey Chhaya) reminds her that in her youth she had done something similar in order to be with her late husband. Instead of the traditional arranged marriage, Dev is permitted to marry the woman of his choice, Western/modern style. The film concludes by demonstrating that those who live with the rules of cultural games also influence the modification of those rules, a concept made palpable when we see Muriel behind the hotel desk and Sonny and his fiancée riding on his motorbike. The interchange between cultures results in compromise and individual exceptions that eventually lead to changes in the cultures because cultural games are serious games that must be adapted to individual differences and historical change. While the clash can lead to discrimination and war, it can also pave the way for tolerance of the anomalous and for peaceful revolution. Nevertheless, it should be kept in mind that the happy ending of both *Quartet* and *The Best Exotic Marigold Hotel* is an artistic, generic phenomenon: comedies end with marriage or the promise of marriage. History is quite another matter. The audience that responds positively to both of these movies is likely to be charmed by the actors acting as actors in *Quartet* and by a sort of extended holiday in India in *The Best Exotic Marigold Hotel*. The films thus end with the pleasant side of ageing and the beautiful element of India. We all know that in both instances there is also a very negative side of ageing and of entering a foreign environment. The cultural expert might warn us that the process of learning to live with other oldsters and integrating into Indian society is likely to be more difficult than seen here. But the films are not cultural documents – a point to be emphasised throughout this book – but works of art with their own goals that need to be respected as creations in their own right. The pleasure evoked at the end of these films is making a different point from mine about cultures. *Quartet* suggests that old age can bring with it aches, pains, and vertigo, but also wisdom in the form of the capacity to forgive. And *The Best Exotic Marigold Hotel* implies that adapting to life in India can revitalise tired old spirits. I expect our cultural expert would reply: it is pleasant to think so.

Sidewalk drama: Lasse Halström's *Salmon Fishing in the Yemen* (2011) and Sam Raimi's *Spider-Man 2* (2004)

Sidewalk drama, the second term of Geertz's method, requires some explanation. In contrast to drama in a theatre, this event takes place on a sidewalk – an American term for what the British call 'pavement' – or free outdoor public space as opposed to seats paid for in an enclosed theatre. The drama performed is not usually overtly theatrical in that it is habitual behaviour, a man raising his hat to a woman, or ritualistic and/or religious, a march or procession. The fact that it is not rehearsed but 'natural', habitual, or ritualistic marks it as deeply embedded in the culture, usually taken for granted by the locals. Geertz freely admits that the phrase is not his own invention. In fact, he explains, it is becoming more widely applied and less in the depreciatory form of 'mere making' and more as 'making, not faking'. In fact, Geertz explains that he combines two kinds of dramatic theory, that of Victor Turner emphasising the ritualistic and religious, and that of Kenneth Burke, who focuses on the secular and political. Employing his own research on the 'theatre state' of Bali, Geertz explains:

> I am concerned, on the one hand, (the Burkean one) to show how everything from kin group organization, trade, customary law, and water control to mythology, architecture, iconography, and cremation combines to a dramatized form of political theory … On the other hand (the Turner one), as the population at large does not merely view the state's expressions as so many gaping spectators but is caught up bodily in them, and especially in the great mass ceremonies … the sort of 'we surrender and are changed' power of drama to shape experience is the strong force that holds the polity together (29–30).

Geertz notes that 'given the dialectical nature of things, we all need our opponents, and both sorts of approach are essential', concluding this section of the chapter with the assertion that as 'social theory turns from propulsive metaphors (the language of pistons) towards ludic ones (the language of pastimes), the humanities are connected to its arguments not in the fashion of skeptical bystanders but, as the source of its imagery, chargeable accomplices' (Geertz, 26). For Geertz the sidewalk drama has a religious/mythological and a secular/socio-political aspect, that is, it involves rituals that enthral and draw us in plus a political theory that encompasses all aspects of civil society.

Sidewalk drama in Salmon Fishing in the Yemen

The sidewalk drama of *Salmon Fishing in the Yemen* is evident in the title itself, the seemingly preposterous idea of a salmon stream in the middle of the Arabian Desert. The unfolding drama of the film about this project involves secular love, religious faith, and politics. The fisheries expert, Dr Alfred Jones (Ewan McGregor), is ordered by his boss to help Sheikh Muhammad of Yemen (Amr Waked) with his pet project because Patricia Maxwell, the prime minister's press secretary (Kristin Scott Thomas), has decided that she needs to counteract the negative press about bombings in Afghanistan with a positive story about the Middle East. So with scepticism, not to say scorn, Dr Jones reluctantly goes off to meet the sheikh's financial adviser, Harriet (Emily Blunt), explaining to her that to complete this bizarre project would involve an insane amount of money as well as physical and geographical difficulties that are insurmountable.

The drama that is played out first involves not only the arid landscape and the unfortunate fish but also people and the British government. Dr Jones is told by Harriet that the money is available, a conversation that is the beginning of a courtship between them. Jones meets the sheikh at his Scottish salmon-fishing estate, where they share an interest in fly-fishing. And when Dr Jones tells the sheikh that aside from the monumental cost of building a salmon stream in Yemen the physical obstacles are beyond modern science, Muhammad encourages Jones to have more faith. At first, Jones, the scientist, remains sceptical but he ultimately comes to like and respect the sheikh.

Now the cultural problems come into play. In order for the salmon stream to remain viable, the fish must spawn upstream, a characteristic of wild, not farm salmon. But the British government will not permit a large number of native salmon to be transported out of the country. The only recourse is to use farm salmon with the hope – and from a scientific point of view a very vague hope, not to say faith – that they will instinctively swim upstream. Here luck prevails; the fish do spawn, reinforcing the sheikh's assertion that faith is required. However, a Yemeni cultural problem now arises. Local terrorists who believe the project is of no use to the local population open the dam, draining the reservoir full of salmon. Undeterred, the sheikh blames himself for not explaining to the local population that the project was to 'irrigate' the Yemen – not merely to bring in fishing tourism but also to make the desert green – and vows to begin again. Jones and Harriet, now an item, decide to help him with his revised sidewalk drama.

This seemingly zany movie has a cultural purpose. In this regard, it is important to recall that Harriet's first boyfriend was thought to be lost in the Afghanistan war; unexpectedly, he returns, to the delight of the prime minister's press secretary, but Harriet chooses Jones over her past companion. This subplot keeps the negative side of the Middle East, that is, the war on terrorism, in our sights. The film thus suggests that while the differences between Islamic and Western cultures are real and possibly insurmountable, they can sometimes serve a positive purpose, especially when the local people can see the benefits of Western or foreign 'improvements', that is, when presented as a sidewalk drama to and for them. At the end of the film, the sheikh and Jones both realise that they neglected the local community, took for granted that they would understand the benefits that would ensue from the project, well beyond salmon-fishing. They hope and believe that they can convince the locals that the project is in their interest. This decision mutually arrived at by the sheikh and the scientist is an example of cultural interchange. The scientist has learned the need for and the place of faith, and the sheikh sees the need to demonstrate the utility of the project, that is, to prove its worth at least quasi-scientifically to his people.

The film concludes, however, not with a new salmon reservoir but with Jones and Harriet staying on in Yemen together and with a series of comical emails about the stupidity of the prime minister, who tried to take credit for the project, pretending to be a trout fisherman and making a fool of himself. The British political scene is presented in the film by the prime minister's press secretary, Patricia Maxwell. Ruthlessly devoted to promoting the image of the government, she is only interested in ensuring the prominence of the prime minister, insisting that he always appear in the best light and be seen as responsible for all that is positive in the eyes of the electorate. Representing a government in such a way suggests an establishment interested in power for power's sake. Anyone, however principled, who flouts the orders of Patricia Maxwell will be dismissed. Indeed, her authority is made apparent at the beginning of the film when Jones is told by the government, that is, Mrs Maxwell, that he will help the sheikh or lose his government position. By contrast, the sheikh is a man of principles, both secular and religious. And for that reason Jones in the end resigns his government position in order to help rebuild the salmon reservoir. The sceptical Scottish scientist has been deeply influenced by the sheikh's culture. He shares the sheikh's interest in the people and agrees with him that they need to involve the community in their project. And earlier, he had to admit that his belief that the farm salmon would go upstream and spawn was based on faith alone, not scientific evidence.

The change in Jones as he befriends the sheikh, becoming enthusiastic about a project he had earlier characterised as folly, is related to his love for Harriet. Instead of the distant, reserved, objective scientist, Jones develops into someone who cares about others, both Harriet and the sheikh, whose life he saves on two occasions, and the people of Yemen. He even begins to tell jokes against himself, something he shares with the sheikh, who realises that his pet project is regarded as the illusion of a man with more money than sense. Harriet and Jones come together by participating in the sheikh's vision, something of little interest to Mrs Maxwell and the government she represents. The sidewalk drama of *Salmon Fishing in the Yemen* is that what appears as folly in another culture, when experienced as a sidewalk drama and understood as a political theory, may be seen as a realisable vision. Lest we dismiss this image of an Arabian salmon stream as preposterous, we might consider that the average Yemeni may have felt that the American project of putting a man on the moon was no less fantastical. The conclusion of the film, however, does raise a serious question: how can Yemen sustain or even bring to partial fruition the greening of its desert without the aid of Britain or other governments? The sidewalk drama that, we presume, convinces the people of Yemen that the project is in their interest is unlikely to have the same effect upon the British government or any other power with the resources to support this scheme. The film is designed to show that what appears sheer folly may with imagination and faith actually be possible.

Sidewalk drama in Spider-Man 2

The image of Spider-Man swinging through New York City on the strands of his web is a particularly spectacular sidewalk drama. At the end of *Spider-Man*, Peter Parker (Tobey Maguire) has overcome his scruples about being Spider-Man. By the beginning of *Spider-Man 2* he is a cultural hero, a sort of secular saviour. And the predominant image of Spider-Man catapulting between Manhattan skyscrapers is reminiscent of Geertz's image of us in our culture '[as] an animal suspended in webs of significance he himself has spun' (Richter, 1368). The web Spider-Man weaves is of a double nature. Peter Parker struggles to make a living, protect his Aunt May (Rosemary Harris), look after his girlfriend, Mary Jane (Kirsten Dunst), and remain on good terms with his best friend, Harry Osborn (James Franco). But his duties as Spider-Man often result in his neglecting his friends and family, even, at times, alienating them. As Spider-Man he is confronted by Octavius (Alfred Molina), the scientist who loses the ability to detach himself from his fusion machine and becomes a sort of mechanical octopus. Peter's domestic struggles and his confrontation with Octavius are both integral to the culture of New York City. Two elements of this sidewalk drama are particularly pertinent to Geertz's concepts. First, Peter Parker is an integrated member of the society, not an outsider observing. His struggles to keep his job, visit his aunt regularly, and pay the rent for an apartment are typical of those confronting the lowest-paid workers in the city. In these endeavours he is buffeted by the forces we all grapple with in a large city, mainly a shortage of time and money. Fortunately, he is welcome both in Aunt May's lower-middle-class house and in the upper-class Osborne residence. He is thus familiar with all levels of life in the city. The struggle from within leads to the second of Geertz's cultural concepts; the other, according to Geertz, is never totally other but always to be viewed as offering another perspective upon ourselves. The end result of conflict thus can avoid total destruction by seeing ourselves in the other. Even in the case of Octavius, Spider-Man convinces him to disarm himself; in that sense, the villainous other is, to some extent, reintegrated into the culture. And with regard to Mary Jane and Aunt May, Peter comes clean, revealing that he is Spider-Man, confessing to his aunt his role in the death of her husband, his beloved Uncle Ben.

Spider-Man is predominantly preoccupied with a sense of responsibility for his fellow New Yorkers, a belief that he must help everyone in the city in need of assistance. What weighs most heavily on his conscience is the fear that any of his enemies who discovered his identity could seek revenge on Aunt May or Mary Jane, the two people he most loves, or on his best friend, Harry Osborn. He lives a double life to protect these people, and we see two sidewalk dramas. In his everyday life, Peter Parker is a gentle, rather passive young man who is exploited by his employer and ground down by the hard life of the city, he is the ordinary New Yorker, alone among crowds indifferent to him and to one another, just the sort of person who might need the assistance of Spider-Man. As Spider-Man, he flies above all this turmoil but remains aware of it. In an early scene, desperate to deliver pizzas on time, he dons his 'spidey suit' but then interrupts his delivery to save two children playing in the street. The pizzas arrive too late, and he loses his job. And no one will know why. This selflessness in the midst of dog-eat-dog New York City is clearly inspiring, especially to the young: as one of the youngsters on the subway seeing him without his mask explains, 'We need a hero.' The self-reliant, unforgiving culture of the Big Apple needs moral muscle, power with integrity.

Peter finds that in maintaining secrecy he has no life of his own, seldom seeing Aunt May and unwilling to admit his love for Mary Jane. In this state of mind he is surprised at the loss of his spider powers, even contemplating giving up Spider-Man and marrying Mary Jane. He is jolted out of this introverted state when informed that a young child has been left in a burning house. While he has been able to resist the temptation of following police cars, the thought of a trapped child is too much for him; he saves the young child without even resorting to his Spider-Man suit. At this point he discovers that Spider-Man is not a persona he adopts but a part of his being; the temporary loss of his spider powers is psychological, caused by his losing touch temporarily with a part of himself. This portion of the sidewalk drama shows us that Peter's deep sense of social responsibility, a kind of civic love, is the source of what Aunt

May, Mary Jane, and his friends love about him, that is, his concern and care for others, his form of love. We cannot but wonder if Aunt May is a source of this capacity, since even when Peter confesses to being partially responsible for the death of her husband, Aunt May, after recovering from the shock, tells him she loves him as much as ever. The softer side of New York City or at least that of a few of its inhabitants is here dramatised.

The major problem for Peter is Octavius/Doctor Octopus, the scientist enslaved by his own invention. This modern, technological Frankenstein has run amok, threatening not only the lives of Aunt May and Mary Jane but also of all the residents of the city. In order to defeat this monster, Spider-Man must use every bit of his strength and ingenuity, in particular to stop the subway train running off the end of the track. In the struggle, he stops the train but collapses with exhaustion, losing his mask. The passengers revive him, noting with amazement that he is only a boy. And true to his boyish ways, he does not destroy Octavius but convinces him to do away with his own pernicious power. He saves Octavius from the worst of himself, and he alone is able to convince the monster, who knows Peter as his former student, a mere boy. We return to the children on the pizza run and the infant in the burning house. The drama here relates to the notion of the child-hero deep in American culture. Is the source of the appeal of Spider-Man – and it has certainly been successful in that respect – the exhilaration of a boy-man on a giant swing in perhaps the largest, most crowded playground in the world? It certainly is for me. In any event, the sidewalk drama of *Spider-Man 2* is that of a boy saviour reviving the child in us all. Now, at the end, he has become a man and is about to marry Mary Jane. We may well wonder whether as a husband and presumably eventually as a father he will be able to continue or will instead pass on his costume to another boy.

However, from the point of view of culture theory, the film concludes with a subtle irony that reinforces the notion that a vibrant culture comes to terms with, sometimes integrates, but never alienates the other. Peter, who has struggled throughout to avoid any permanent attachment to his beloved Mary Jane because he assumes no woman should have to share the risks and responsibilities of Spider-Man, is surprised when she says 'Don't you think it is about time somebody saved *your* life?' and later, upon hearing the police sirens, 'Go get them, tiger.' For a change, Spider-Man is the other who needs to learn that cultures need and thrive on difference. We are left to wonder: is this new relationship between Mary Jane and Spider-Man sidewalk drama or reality?

Behavioural text: Jon Favreau's *Iron Man 2* (2010) and Shane Black's *Iron Man 3* (2013)

Geertz explains that what he means by behavioural text is action or behaviour that needs to be read or interpreted as if it were words, that is, as an extended version of body language, where our actions and conduct can be interpreted as an unrehearsed drama not intended for presentation:

> The great virtue of the extension of the notion of text beyond things written on paper or carved into stone is that it trains attention on precisely this phenomenon: on how the inscription of action is brought about, what its vehicles are and how they work, and on what the fixation of meaning from the flow of events – history from what happened, thought from thinking, culture from behavior – implies for sociological interpretation. To see social institutions, social customs, social changes as in some sense 'readable' is to alter our whole sense of what such interpretation is and shift it towards modes of thought rather more familiar to the translator, the exegete, or the iconographer than to the test giver, the factor analyst, or the pollster (31).

For Geertz, behavioural texts involve the process of writing or inscribing and the product, the behavioural moment that leads to the text being created and the text itself. In fact, the separation of these two elements of the 'readable' is to be avoided:

> The study of inscriptions is severed from the study of inscribing, the study of fixed meaning is severed from the study of the social processes that fix it. The result is a double narrowness. Not only is the extension of text analysis to nonwritten materials blocked, but so is the application of sociological to written ones. The repair of this split and the integration of the study of how texts are built, how the said is rescued from its saying, into the study of social phenomena – Apache jokes, English meals, African cult sermons, American high

schools, Indian caste, or Balinese widow burning, ... are what the
'new philology', or whatever else it eventually comes to be called, is
all about (32).

Behavioural text in Iron Man 2

The study of behavioural texts by what Geertz calls 'proponents of
"life as a text"' tends to examine 'imaginative forms: jokes, prov-
erbs, popular arts' (33). Popular art is an apt description of *Iron Man
2*. My focus will be on *Iron Man 2* and *Iron Man 3* because *Iron
Man* sets the context for the sequels. Tony Stark has finally admitted that he is Iron Man and boasted that because the capabilities of
Iron Man are owned solely by Stark Industries, the United States
for the first time in history can guarantee world peace. However,
Iron Man 2 shows that others can duplicate the technology of Iron
Man, while *Iron Man 3* demonstrates that world peace cannot be
obtained through armaments alone, even those of Iron Man. Both
these sequels exemplify Geertz's concept of a behavioural text.

To quickly refresh our minds, *Iron Man* ends with Tony Stark
(Robert Downey Jr) destroying the stolen arc reactor. Now he can
for the first time admit that he is Iron Man and claim that he alone
has the 'weapon of weapons' that no one else can duplicate. Hence
Iron Man 2 begins with Tony asserting that Stark Industries has
successfully 'privatised' military arms for peace. In the next scene of
Iron Man 2, Tony is subpoenaed before a congressional committee
to be confronted by a US senator demanding that he hand over Iron
Man, a lethal weapon illegally held in private hands. Tony refuses,
asserting that Iron Man is a part of him, not a separate weapon.
Departing from the Senate chamber with a flourish, Tony boasts
that the senator should thank him for permanently establishing
peace, then drives off complacently in an expensive sports car to
engage in one of his favourite pastimes, race-car driving. Here he
is confronted by a form of terrorism, well beyond what he experienced in Afghanistan, in the form of the personal animus of Ivan
Vanko (Mickey Rourke), a Russian who is avenging an injustice
that he believes was done to his father by Stark's father. Moreover,
since Vanko's father was originally a colleague of Stark's father, Ivan
has technical prowess nearly equal to that of Tony. Ivan confronts
Tony on the racetrack, very nearly defeating Iron Man. Later, when
Ivan is incarcerated, Tony admits to being impressed with how close

the Russian came to equalling the capabilities of Iron Man. Tony, the cocky, prosperous American entrepreneur, remains confident of his superiority over the rough-spoken proletarian Russian engineer. Certain of the superiority of his weaponry and that it cannot be duplicated, Tony decides to hand over the management of the company to Pepper Potts (Gwyneth Paltrow), enabling him to turn his energies to repairing his war wound, in particular, to finding a replacement for palladium, the element that is temporarily keeping him alive but gradually killing him.

Meanwhile, Justin Hammer, Tony's competitor, whom he holds in contempt, has managed to steal Ivan from prison and convinced him to use his expertise to build an alternative to Iron Man, one that Justin can sell to the US Department of Defense, resulting in huge profits and, even more important to him, one-upping Tony. Ivan, however, has his own plans, rigging up a series of robots with a new kind of software designed to defeat Iron Man. The ensuing battle between Ivan's robots and Iron Man is a kind of behavioural text. Once battle begins it becomes clear that Ivan has no scruples about collateral damage; he is quite willing to kill innocent civilians in order to destroy Tony. While Ivan focuses solely on killing Tony and his allies by any means, even at the cost of masses of bystanders, Tony is more restricted in his strategy because he insists on avoiding civilian casualties. Ivan's innovation, booby-trapped robots, a sort of advanced version of IEDs (improvised explosive devices), are his secret weapons; once the robots have been disarmed/'killed' they become timed explosive devices blowing up within seconds, Ivan assumes, the unsuspecting 'victors'.

We thus come to understand from this clash of the Russian and American techies that Tony, although admittedly a narcissist, values individuality, risking his life to protect not only himself but also innocent bystanders. The battle becomes a behavioural text because if read carefully it shows us that Tony is saved by and saves his friends while Ivan is alone and thereby defeated. The battle demonstrates that the war cannot be won by weapons and technology alone; friends and allies are also required. Even Justin Hammer (Sam Rockwell), the unscrupulous entrepreneur, does not set out to kill innocents; his weapons are overpriced and relatively worthless on the battlefield – we recall his cherished 'Cohiba' bullet bouncing off Ivan's armour like a bit of tin – as Tony had predicted. And in the end the authorities arrest Justin for his venture into illegal robotics.

The text here is a clash of cultures, the United States that values, perhaps even overvalues, individuality, versus Russia that will not compromise its objective for any individual or for the principle of individuality. The recent Russian bombing of Syria suggests that little has changed. The film thus ends with Pepper showing her love and respect for Tony who has transferred his self-love not only to his friends and colleagues but also to society in general, not a concern we ever see expressed by Ivan Vanko. Nonetheless, *Iron Man 2* concludes with Tony being regarded by the establishment as a loose cannon, someone to be consulted but not included in the team, or, in the words of a US senator, an 'annoying little prick'. And here the film moves beyond being a behavioural text of American versus Russian culture. Tony is annoying to the American establishment because he insists on his independence; Iron Man is not for him an invention or a weapon but a part of his being. The corollary of this 'narcissism' is that he assumes responsibility for Iron Man as he does for himself. While the US government sees this attitude as selfish and illegal, we shall be shown it in a different light. Justin Hammer is more to the liking of the establishment because he will do what they want so long as he is sufficiently well paid. The American system has its own loopholes – places for entrepreneurial explosive devices like (those of) Justin – but the concept of protecting the innocent, that is, the law, remains an important counterbalance that is seldom present in Russia. The problem left unresolved at the end of *Iron Man 2* is that even if Tony does eventually defeat Ivan, does that really resolve the problem or will someone else from an alien culture try to defeat Tony with some more recent advancement in weapon technology.

Behavioural text in Iron Man 3

Iron Man 3 turns to the problem of the nature of the enemy; the film is framed by Stark's asserting at the beginning and end that 'we make our own demons'. In *Iron Man 2*, Ivan's resources are provided from within, by Hammer, an American competitor of Stark Industries. Hammer is a rather ineffectual rival, as is demonstrated in the final confrontation with Ivan when, as we have seen, Hammer's prize weapon fails even to dent the armour of the Russian. The real enemy is altogether more formidable. In this final part of the trilogy, the enemy within, Aldrich Killian (Guy Pearce), is far more effective than Hammer, and his animosity derives not from Tony's father but from Tony's own arrogant behaviour. When he had just started out as a young inventor, Aldrich wished to share his new ideas with Stark enterprises. Tony promised to meet him but never showed up, and we eventually learn that Mandarin, the public face of the enemy, is merely a puppet for Aldrich. The behavioural text that emerges is the process by which Tony Stark creates his own demon. Tony believes that Iron Man is the weapon to end all weapons because it cannot be duplicated and will remain in his responsible hands. Aldrich demonstrates that he is wrong, creating a weapon that is equally lethal, perhaps even more so in that it often results in misfires, accidental acts of terrorism that even Aldrich cannot completely control.

Moreover, Tony has his own inner demons to confront. In addition to the palladium that is literally eating away at him, he is subject to bouts of anxiety as if some unconscious element of his psyche is signalling that he needs help. Aid will come in the surprising form of Nick Fury (Samuel L. Jackson), head of SHIELD (Strategic Homeland Intervention, Enforcement and Logistics Division), the government CIA-type agency, who points out to Stark that he has not made any progress against Mandarin on his own. Part of the process of discovery of the demon within is the recognition that everyone needs help from others, indeed from the community itself represented by Fury and his agents, one of whom is, to Tony's surprise, Pepper Potts' personal assistant, Natalie Rushman (Scarlett Johansson). Both agents warn Tony about the nature of the enemy, called Mandarin, who, as we have already noted, proves to be merely a puppet for Aldrich. The anxiety attacks seem to derive from Tony's childhood, something that becomes manifest when a young boy becomes one of his important allies. While investigating an act of accidental terrorism – one of Mandarin's misfires – in rural Tennessee, he befriends a young boy not unlike himself as a youngster who helps put him back in touch with his own childhood. Since Fury had pointed out that Tony has a distorted view of his father, he revisits some films made by Stark Senior before his death that provide the means by which Tony finds a substitute for the palladium in his chest, enabling him to live a normal life. Tony remarks to himself that even in his grave his father remains his teacher. And at the end of the film the boy in Tennessee finds that his garage has been turned into a high-tech lab, Tony's way of saying thanks for his help. Re-establishing himself with his father and his own childhood helps humanise Tony, enabling him come to terms with his own inner demons.

In the great final battle with Aldrich, Tony meets his match and is eventually saved by Pepper, who dispatches the arch-enemy with a single blow. Even under the influence of Aldrich's terrible brain-washing technique, Pepper remains committed to her love for Tony, always aware of his repressed love for her. Similarly, Tony's old friend from *Iron Man*, Rhodey (Don Cheadle), remains at Tony's side during the battle. Reading this battle as a behavioural text, we understand the need to come to terms with our own demons if we are to confront those of our culture. In this regard, the ulti-mate framing device of the trilogy seen in the credits shows us the intended audience is someone who has gone to sleep; we discover that the entire Iron Man trilogy has been a story told to Dr Bruce Banner who, understandably after nearly six hours, has nodded off. The point of this epilogue in the final credits is that this cultural cinema epic is really only Tony's story, one individual's attempt to come to terms with demons within and without. It is therefore a behavioural text in that we now see not only the story but the orig-inal audience for the story, the story as an unfolding event and as a finished product, the movie just completed. It is, as Geertz would say, one person's story, a tale with a singular signature, an inter-pretation that points outwardly to the culture and inwardly to the storyteller.

The warm centre of *Iron Man 3* is Ben Kingsley's cameo part as Mandarin, the name adopted by the arch-terrorist who is himself terrorised by Aldrich. In a fine Janus-faced performance Mandarin presents himself on video as the toughest of warriors, fearless and without scruples; when seen in person he is a drug addict afraid of his own shadow. The arch-enemy is thus seen as not only of our own making but also a projection of our own fears, for even Aldrich could not pose a threat to the establishment without the collusion of the vice-president of the United States, who is deter-mined to usurp the position of the president. This text of *Iron Man 3* illustrates another key principle of Geertz's anthropological the-ory, namely that to understand the other we must adopt the other's view of ourselves. The very name Mandarin suggests a stereotyp-ical 'other', a notion exploited by Aldrich, who is as American as Tony. And Mandarin's performance is a sort of sub-behavioural text of a paper tiger, a projection of our own fears, a projection onto a foreign, exotic other culture, an enemy who is in fact very home-grown.

In the end, Tony starts a new life, beginning – to Pepper's delight – by destroying all the Iron Man suits and discarding his old palladium 'heart'. Discovering the demon within himself and within his culture has brought him to peace with himself and with that aspect of Iron Man represented by the boy in rural Tennessee. Always Iron Man, as he asserts, he can now move on to a normal married life with Pepper because that humanity, that capacity to love another, has enabled him to come to terms with himself and his culture. Tony has undergone a kind of sea change. Geertz, we are reminded, concluded that this new relationship between anthropology and the other social sciences and the humanities represents a 'sea change' in both directions. And Pepper, who began as the curator of Tony's art collection, represents the humanities in contrast to the scientific technology of Iron Man. At the end of *Iron Man 3* the humanities are put into power in place of science, a bold experiment that has yet to be tried and tested.

> The refiguration of social theory represents, or will if it continues, a sea change in our notion not so much of what knowledge is but of what it is we want to know. Social events do have causes and social institutions effects, but it just may be that the road to discovering what we assert in asserting this lies less through postulating forces and measuring them than through noting expressions and inspecting them (Geertz, 34).

The social scientist is thus encouraged to adopt the ways of the humanities, particularly the interpretive techniques of literary criticism. The result of this new rapprochement will also significantly change the humanities, specifically how we do literary analysis:

> If the social technologist's notion of what a social scientist is is brought into question by all this concern with sense and signification, even more so is the cultural watchdog notion of what a humanist is. The specialist without spirit dispensing policy nostrums goes, but the lectern sage dispensing approved judgments does as well. The relation between thought and action in social life can no more be conceived of in terms of wisdom than it can in terms of expertise (Geertz, 35).

The literary critic can no longer count on the old absolutes, the traditional themes of Matthew Arnold's 'culture': we must enter the treacherous waters off the cliffs of Dover, confronting 'anarchy' in our own culture and that of others. Our inner demons are only to be understood by comparing them to those of other cultures and seeing how others perceive us – and our demons. The literary critic is set a new task, that of the anthropological literary critic, one that involves a new method as well as an expanded subject matter. In the chapters that follow we shall examine various views about how this new goal can be achieved.

2 Hayden White and history as mixture of fact and fiction

Hayden White, like Geertz, believes in the interpretive turn, but for his discipline of history the element of fiction is central. White makes clear that the facts of history are not sufficient; alone they lead to a chronicle, what Benedetto Croce called 'one damned thing after another' (189). Weaving the strands or facts of history into a narrative involves elements of fiction: to make a story out of the bare bones of history is a literary craft. The first part of this chapter considers the art of historical narrative in the context of Mr Holmes *and* The West Wing. *White goes on to explain that one key element in the story of history is the concept of plot or what he calls 'emplotment'. This concept is considered in the next section, in conjunction with* The Second Best Marigold Hotel *and* House of Cards. *Emplotment can only be successfully achieved by use of tropology and culture, elements of rhetorical style necessary for history. In the third section,* Frozen *and* The Railway Man *serve as examples.*

Hayden White, Professor Emeritus at the University of California, Santa Cruz, enters the literary sphere from the point of view of the story, the narrative element that distinguishes history from chronicle, what Benedetto Croce so aptly described as 'one damned thing after another'. The historical narrative provides cohesion, coherence and human interest for the facts that a chronicle merely records. And White makes quite clear that the narrative aspect of history is distinctly literary.

> In short, historical discourse should not be considered as a special case of the 'workings of our minds' in its efforts to know reality or to describe it, but rather as a special kind of language use, which like

metaphoric speech, symbolic language, and allegorical representation, always means more than it literally says, says something other
than what it seems to mean, and reveals something of the world at the
cost of concealing something else (Cohen, *Future* 25).

White goes on to explain that the story that develops from the historian's use of language in this way is interpretive and therefore never
definitive.

> It is the metaphoric nature of the great classics of historiography
> that explains why none of them has ever 'wrapped up' a historical
> problem definitively, but has always 'opened up' a prospect of the
> past that inspires more study. It is this fact that authorizes us to
> classify historical discourse primarily as interpretation rather than
> as explanation or description, and above all as a kind of writing,
> which instead of pacifying our will to know, stimulates us to ever
> more research, ever more discourse, ever more writing. (Cohen,
> *Future* 25).

We would be mistaken if we assume that while giving considerable
weight to the literary aspect of history White does not give equal
weight to the factual or non-literary element, which, he emphasises,
is key at the research stage for the historian.

> None of this implies that we should not discriminate between the
> activity of historical research ... and that of historical writing ... In
> the research phase of their work, historians are concerned to discover
> the truth about the past and to recover information either forgot-
> ten, suppressed, or obscured, and, of course, to make of it whatever
> sense they can. But between the research phase, which is really quite
> indistinguishable from that of a journalist or a detective, and the
> completion of a written history, a number of important transform-
> ative operations must be performed in which the figurative aspect of
> the historian's thought is intensified rather than diminished (Cohen,
> *Future* 25).

For White the distinction between fiction and history remains, but
the border is less absolute, more blurred because the historian cannot produce a narrative without an element of fiction.

Historical writing as a narrative: Bill Condon's *Mr Holmes* (2015) and Aaron Sorkin's *The West Wing*, series 1, episode 1 (1999)

Historical writing as a narrative in Mr Holmes

Since White describes the research phase of history as indistinguishable from that of a detective, I begin with a recent Sherlock Holmes film. *Mr Holmes* is the story of Sherlock Holmes (Ian McKellen) in his latter years when he retires to the countryside to attend to his beehives. Although no longer available to solve crimes, Holmes is haunted by his last case, one he has been struggling to write up since Watson, the writer, according to the film, of this particular Sherlock Holmes story, has recently died, leaving an account that Holmes believes is inaccurate, since it omits all mention of his struggle with his sense of responsibility for the unfortunate outcome of the case. At his advanced age Mr Holmes struggles not only because his memory is not what it was but also because he regards the final outcome as a personal failure, a fact not made clear in Watson's narrative, 'The Adventures of the Dove Grey Glove'. The story, we learn in the film, involves a woman who has lost two children *in utero* and mourns them in ways her husband finds objectionable, if not quite mad. She communes with the spirits of the infants by way of her music teacher, a clairvoyant. The husband forbids any more music lessons, fearing that she has formed a pact with the Devil or been taken advantage of by an impostor.

Holmes' investigation shows his shrewd psychological insight. He follows her as she forges cheques in her husband's name and cashes them, buys poison from a chemist, visits a lawyer to find out the details of her husband's will, and looks carefully at train schedules. In the course of following her, Holmes realises that when he loses her momentarily she waits for him. He therefore surmises that she is trying to convince him that she plans to murder her husband. He decides to confront her to make clear that he recognises that her activities are merely a subterfuge, not a plan to murder her husband but a means of calling attention to herself and her despair over the infant deaths. Admitting that he is correct, she explains that she has been waiting for someone who understands her as he alone does, pleading with him to spend the rest of his life with her as a kindred spirit. Understanding that in her emotional state these strange activities – without any criminal intent – merely represent her own eccentric way of trying to come to terms with the deaths of her two children, Holmes is sympathetic to her plight. Once she has recovered from the shock of his keen insight into her inner being, Holmes in a distant if delicate way advises her to return to her loving husband. Shortly thereafter, she commits suicide by throwing herself in front of a train. Holmes is so haunted by her death that he retires, believing that the only crime in this final case is his own in not preventing her suicide. As a man committed to the facts, he seems capable of marvellous insight into the motives and, particularly in this instance, into the psychological strategies for covering up these motives but singularly unable to come to terms with his own motives and subterfuges. Clearly, Holmes has fallen in love with the woman but remains for some time oblivious to his own feelings.

Now in retirement, Holmes racks his brain for details of this past case to write it down as history – to replace Watson's account that is, in his view, less accurate and more fanciful. The film thus creates a new role for Holmes; he is no longer merely the detective with Dr Watson to take notes and write up the tale. Now he is the writer, this particular case is as much about him, his inner being, as about the woman with the dove grey glove. In short, Mr Holmes is made by the film into a historian, specifically, an autobiographer. Moreover, as gradually becomes clear, he is trying not only, as he puts it at the outset, to set the record straight, sort out the facts, but also, as he later admits to the two other main characters in the film, to expiate his guilt concerning his failure to save the woman's life.

Upon first arriving at the country cottage, Holmes is a crotchety, unhappy old man. The source of his unhappiness is that he refuses to consider anything but the facts, thereby eliminating himself, his psychological motives, except for what he regards as the fact that he deserted a woman in her hour of need. During his struggles to recall the details of this case, he becomes interested in the son of his housekeeper, Roger (Milo Parker) who is observant, intelligent and interested in Sherlock Holmes and detective work. Gradually they form a grandfatherly friendship, with Roger learning both about detecting and keeping bees. Holmes continues to struggle with the narrative of his case because, as he explains, he has little interest in the imaginary or fictive, and the necessary facts his ailing mind finds ever more elusive. Fortunately, Roger comes to understand Holmes so well that he knows how to help stimulate his memory. In particular, he discovers in Watson's bureau the dove grey glove.

At this point it is clear that the boy and Holmes have made companions of one another and that in spite of himself the old man is happier with the boy than we have seen him at any point in the film. Nevertheless, Holmes remains unable to recapture in words the case of the woman with the dove grey glove; clearly, his effort to write history with only the facts is doomed to failure.

At the same time we see his affection for the boy increasing. As a reward for finding the glove, Holmes teaches Roger how to look after the bees, even at times allowing him to tend to them on his own. Eventually Holmes tells the boy another story of his past. In 1947, just after the end of the war, Holmes was invited to visit Japan by Tamiki Umezaki (Hiroyuki Sanada), whose father, a Japanese diplomat and great admirer of Conan Doyle's Sherlock Holmes stories, became a spy for and remained in England, never returning to his family in Japan. The film shows Holmes during this visit again demonstrating keen psychological insight into another person. Although this man professes to be a great fan of Sherlock, Mr Holmes realises that the copy of the stories supposedly cherished for years by this man was in fact a library book, not a family heirloom. This man, not unlike the woman with the dove grey glove, is hiding his real motives. Finally, Tamiki confesses that he had no interest in Sherlock Holmes but hoped to find out something about his father. At that point Holmes explains that he did not know his father. Later, as his affection for Roger helps him come to terms with his inner self, he recalls being summoned by Mycroft, his brother, a government minister, to interview Tamiki's father to help decide if he would be a trustworthy spy. Only at that point does he realise that his decision to validate his brother's decision to use the father as a spy had a lasting effect on the son, an effect that, like his advice to the grieving mother, was something he did not give due consideration at the time. The personal histories of the woman who committed suicide and the son of the Japanese diplomat have both been affected by Mr Holmes' refusal to consider anything other than what he calls the facts. Although conscience-stricken on both counts, Holmes is trapped by his insistence on avoiding the non-factual, his own inner world of the imagination, of the fictions that inhabit our psyches.

But, as White would have predicted, Holmes' obsession with the past is interrupted by a crisis in the present; history almost always involves an intermingling of the past and the present. Protecting the beehive from wasps, Roger has been stung repeatedly, is in a coma, and may not survive. Distraught, Holmes arrives at the cottage to find his housekeeper, Mrs Munro (Laura Linney), the mother of Roger, attempting to set fire to the beehive. When she accuses him of stealing her son, he falls on his knees in tears, confessing his grandfatherly love for the boy. Realising that he is sincere, she begins to pity him. As they both calm down, Holmes notices that although at the beehive, they are surrounded by wasps, not bees. Now the great Sherlock's brain goes to work; he infers that clearly Roger was trying to protect the bees from the wasps, and, as he recalls from an earlier incident, Roger is particularly sensitive to wasp stings. Together, mother and surrogate grandfather burn the wasp nest with some mutual satisfaction. For the first time, Mrs Munro feels some affection for the poor old duffer. After this emotional catharsis, Holmes confesses to her that he failed the woman with the grey dove glove by not accepting her love and that he was so detached from his Japanese acquaintance that he forgot that he had met his father during the war and was consulted about his suitability as a spy. Now he realises he must respond to the love of Roger before it is too late. As an act of contrition and reparation, he wills his entire estate to her and Roger and writes a letter to the son of the Japanese diplomat/spy describing his father as a brave, honourable man, an assertion that, he later explains to Roger, is fiction, presumably his first foray into that realm.

Although Mr Holmes only reconciles himself to the mingling of fact with fiction at the end of the film as a result of guilt, the film itself from the outset combines both spheres to show that stories, compelling or interesting narratives, cannot but involve both fiction and fact – if the original Holmes is seen as a sort of historical personage. Mr Holmes of the film feels compelled to tell white lies about the Japanese spy to help repair some of the damage to the son. He now accepts partial responsibility for the son being deprived of his father throughout the war. In this way Holmes begins to come to terms with his past, to be a better autobiographer, a process completed by his making Roger and Mrs Munro his heirs.

The film has employed fiction throughout, straying from the original to demonstrate how a story, even a historical story, cannot do without some fiction. The *donnée* of the film, Holmes' guilt about his last case, and the case itself, not to mention the death of Watson and many other details are not to be found in the original Sherlock Holmes stories. However, some facts, that is, details derived from the Conan Doyle source, remain: Holmes himself remains deeply observant, detached but aware of all of the complexities of human events from the psychological to the sociological, the amateur scientist weighing the evidence, the man of infinite curiosity. In that sense the film is historical, not merely fanciful. For it provides us with an explanation of Sherlock Holmes' ability to unravel crimes motivated by clever, devious people. The implication is that he had to have been capable of love and empathy to understand the motives of criminals, but in Conan Doyle's version that all remains implicit or repressed and certainly is never applied to himself. Of course, it is possible to argue that Conan Doyle's Sherlock Holmes was more a persona than a person, that for Conan Doyle the analysis of the crime was more important than Sherlock's inner being. Perhaps. Then the film can be said to have made the persona into a person showing what kind of human being is capable of unravelling mysteries like that of the case of the dove grey glove. In any event, 'Mr Holmes' fulfils a historical purpose, although in this case it is a literary historical one, and fiction is a necessary ingredient of that mix.

As White had predicted, this approach to the great Victorian sleuth opens up new possibilities for Sherlock Holmes fans and scholars. Do Holmes' personal feelings of love and empathy relate to the other stories, and, if so, why has this side of the great detective been neglected until now? These and many other new prospects appear on the horizon, for the best history instead of 'wrapping up' 'opens up' the subject. Certainly, the wonderful variety of Ian McKellen's facial expressions opens up a new 'vista', to employ White's term, of interest: a fine but ageing brain struggling with memory loss and advancing senility. Here art differs from history, for McKellen's Mr Holmes can investigate other cases than those found in Conan Doyle whose stories have become a document of history and must be adhered to for purposes of historical accuracy. In that respect, the film moves beyond history by way of history. For the film asserts that Mr Holmes, as a person or persona, has exceeded Conan Doyle's narratives. Conan Doyle created him but has, in a sense, bequeathed him to his readers and admirers. He belongs to us, and we can, if we wish to indulge in sheer fiction, make of him what we will, even imagining what he would be like as an old man in retirement tending his bees in the countryside.

Mr Holmes straddles fact and fiction, as in 'faction', itself a blurred genre, but it serves to demonstrate that stories made of at least some historical facts need fiction, in varying amounts admittedly, to provide cohesion and coherence to the narrative.

Historical writing as a narrative in The West Wing, *series 1, episode 1*

The opening episode of this extremely successful series appears to be an introduction to daily life in the West Wing, the offices or working side, as opposed to the residential quarters, of the White House. In fact, the setting for the series is the actual West Wing or at least a set that is so like it that even those who know the West Wing would believe it to be the place itself. And that is perhaps the first statement that the series makes: this television show, although completely fictional, is about daily life in the West Wing, that is, about a real or actual site that represents the inner workings of the United States presidency. Fiction here is in the service of fact or, more accurately, probable reality: what is an average day like in the West Wing. Very busy, it would appear.

The president (Martin Sheen) has had a bicycle accident; Josh (Bradley Whitford), the deputy chief of staff, has in a television interview insulted an important political figure; 1,200 illegal Cuban immigrants are struggling in the ocean to reach Florida; Sam (Rob Lowe), deputy communications officer, has had sexual relations with a woman who, he did not know at the time, is a call girl. Many of these incidents, not resolved in this episode, are to be pursued later in the series. Lest we assume that this is merely a chronicle of quotidian White House life, Josh's gaffe on television is the main topic of this episode.

The incident involves the relationship between what is called the 'Christian right', a minority but powerful interest group, and the political party of the president, who is a Democrat. Josh has insulted a key member of this religious group, a woman named Mary Marsh (Annie Corley), who takes exception to Josh's reference to God, asserting that she does not worship the same deity. Josh replies: 'Your God is busy being indicted for tax fraud.' The problem is that the Christian right includes important supporters of the president, and the last thing he wants is for any of his people to insult them. Three scenes in this episode suggest how this religious group has achieved public attention and political muscle. In the first scene, set in a cocktail lounge, Sam is being quizzed by a journalist while flirting with a beautiful woman across the room who will turn out to be a call girl. We are left to ponder whether she is attracted to him for his good looks, his position of power, or a combination of both. The second scene occurs when Josh lunches with an ex-girlfriend who now works for a senator with ambitions to be president. He discovers that she is 'dating' him, someone who is very likely married with a family, since few senators can be elected if single. Third, Sam has at the last minute been given an assignment to give a talk about the history of the White House to a group of fourth-graders who have won an essay contest on this topic and have been awarded this visit to the seat of their government. These scenes make clear that while Washington, DC is full of various forms of corruption and questionable ethics, something that most of us take for granted, the young primary-school children of the United States regard it with the highest respect. Clearly, this general atmosphere helps explain how the Christian right publicly opposed to the questionable moral behaviour of those at the heart of government can gain such prominence in present-day American politics.

Fortunately, keeping a cool head, Josh's superior, Toby Ziegler (Richard Schiff), arranges a meeting between the leaders of the religious group so that Josh can apologise, putting the matter to rest. Although Mary Marsh seems to accept the apology, she wants to 'deal' as she puts it, that is, expects a favour in return, such as banning condoms in schools. She then goes on to make reference to what she calls 'fast-talking' advisers at the meeting. Josh's superior, clearly himself Jewish, recognises this remark as anti-Semitic, making clear to Mary that he objects to her inference. At this climactic point, with tempers at fever pitch, the president enters with the aid of a walking stick, commanding the respect of everyone. With the expertise of a seasoned politician, he greets everyone, immediately understanding that the temperature of the conversation is running high, interrupts to tell a story – a story within a story that contains, in my view, the key to the episode.

He begins by pointing out that his wife has always advised him never to do anything in haste when angry but in spite of this advice and although very upset he went off hurriedly on his bike, ran into a tree, refused to be helped to his feet, and fell flat on his face. Now with his audience in his grip, he explains the source of his anger. His twelve-year-old granddaughter had somewhat precociously made a public statement concerning abortion, supporting women's right to choose for themselves – a position vehemently opposed by the Christian right. As a result of speaking out on this issue, she received in the post from a group calling itself 'Lamb of God' a rag doll with a knife in it. When the head of the religious interest group asserts that he has nothing to do with 'Lamb of God', the president replies, 'crap', demanding that he 'fix it'. The president then makes clear to them that until this matter is remedied they have nothing further to say to one another and orders them to leave immediately. When Mary Marsh remarks tartly, 'We know our way out', the president replies, 'Then do it, now.' The high tempers here on both sides of the issue make clear the passions of power, passions that range from the president's love for his granddaughter to Josh's remark about Mary Marsh's 'God'.

The point of the president's story – and the key to the entire episode – is that morality is a two-edged sword; it may result in punishment of the guilty or victimisation of the innocent, as in this instance of the twelve-year-old granddaughter. Absolute or dogmatic judgement in these matters can result in injustice. For instance, Sam as a single young man has committed no crime in having sexual relations with a consenting unmarried adult; he could not know that she was a call girl and only found out subsequently by accident. Nevertheless, if this matter became public knowledge his political career could be ruined. Similarly, we do not know the specifics of the relationship between Josh's ex-girlfriend and the senator. Their dating may be purely platonic or, if not, the senator may intend to divorce and remarry. The story of the rag doll with a knife suggests that the West Wing world is a mixture not only of power and corruption but also of great political possibilities and unexpected traps and quagmires that may have little to do with personal innocence or guilt. Life in this world is insecure and often short-lived: angry accusations like those of Josh or cruel gestures like that represented by the pierced rag doll are equally to be avoided.

The episode ends with the president cautioning Josh never to speak like that again, suggesting that his words were as dangerous as the action of the person who sent the doll. The story that is woven from the strands of chronicle here shows that life in the West Wing is precarious and that language in the political arena can be as dangerous as aggressive actions, a point hinted at earlier when the woman on the treadmill explaining to her co-exerciser that her workout time, from 5 to 6 a.m., is her personal time, is interrupted by her pager, trips up, and disappears from view. A similar fate nearly happens to both Sam and Josh, not to mention the president himself. As White had led us to understand, this narrative is based not merely upon facts but upon interpretation: the 'Christian right' is seen as a group – although viewed by the President's advisers as 'stupid' – capable of causing political difficulties for the president and his party. Finally, although every detail of this episode is fictional, the point made has clear applicability to reality: extremism on both the right and the left endangers the entire political process. The fictional story about the West Wing provides a plausible image of quotidian life at the heart of the American capital. In that sense this episode illustrates White's point about how fiction aids truth or historical reality. The series also has the 'poetic licence' that is denied to a more traditional form of history; a future episode might wish to display an ideal Washington world without corruption and aggressive ambitions. Unlike history, *The West Wing*, as a work of art, can choose to straddle history and fiction, as in this episode, or to move wholly into fiction quite apart from historical fact, departing from the West Wing as we know it, imagining a utopian American capital. The boundaries between fiction and history remain but are less distinct than might have been assumed. The difference between the two often involves interpretation, since even the most conscientious historian cannot be restricted only to what actually happened but will have to resort to filling in the gaps of the narrative with probable occurrences. Probability is contestable; facts are not.

Historical 'emplotment': John Madden's *The Second Best Exotic Marigold Hotel* (2015) and Beau Willimon's *House of Cards*, series 1, episode 1 (2013)

White describes the process of moving from chronicle to history as follows:

> In the passage from a study of an archive to the composition of discourse to its translation into a written form, historians must employ the same strategies of linguistic figuration used by imaginative writers …

> The kind of interpretation typically produced by the historical discourse
> is that which endows what would otherwise remain only a chronolog-
> ically ordered series of events with the formal coherency of the kind of
> plot structures met with in narrative fiction (Cohen, *Future* 25–6).

Consequently, White argues that the historical procedure of com-
position is less marked by logical progression than by what he calls
'tropological' movement:

> If, when viewed from the perspective of a logician, the typical histor-
> ical discourse must be seen as having the structure of an enthymeme
> rather than a true syllogism, it is because turns more tropical than
> logical preside over its endowment of a series of events with the struc-
> tural coherence of a plot form and its endowment of a set of facts
> with whatever meaning it is supposed to possess. Indeed, it is only by
> troping, rather than by logical deduction, that the kinds of past events
> we would wish to call 'historical' can (first) be *represented* as having
> the order of a chronicle, (secondly) be *transformed* by emplotment
> into an identifiable story with a beginning, middle and end phases,
> and (thirdly) be constituted as the subject of whatever formal argu-
> ments may be adduced to establish their 'meaning' – cognitive, ethi-
> cal, or aesthetic, as the case may be (Cohen, *Future* 26).

Historical 'emplotment' in The Second Best Exotic Marigold Hotel

The notion of emplotment and the sort of troping that results is
exemplified in *The Second Best Exotic Marigold Hotel*. The plot
of this sequel involves the attempt of Sonny Kapoor (Dev Patel),
the owner of the first Best Exotic Marigold Hotel, with the help
of Muriel Donnelly (Maggie Smith), his assistant, to convince a
California businessman to invest in a second hotel. After some discussion, the businessman indicates that his decision will be based on
the report of an inspector who will not identify him or herself when
visiting the hotel. The issue at the outset of the film is financial trust.
Is the new hotel what Muriel and Sonny say it is, and is it worth
the investment they need? As we shall see, trust of a more personal
sort is important for all the guests at the hotel. Trust is also crucial
for the historian. Once it is understood that the historian does not
merely present the facts but weaves them into a story or fiction,

then the reader must trust that the historian's finished product does justice to the facts and does not exclude facts that might undermine his narrative. And White argues that one means the historian uses to convince his audience to trust his account is emplotment, the same means Sonny and Muriel use to convince their potential investor of the financial viability of their second Best Marigold Hotel.

The future visit of the inspector who will assess the financial viability of the hotel directly affects all the hotel residents. Although Guy Chambers (Richard Gere) pretends to be a writer on holiday, Sonny immediately believes that he is the inspector; his presence clearly represents a financial turning point for Sonny and Muriel. In fact, all the residents of the hotel are involved in personal turning points involving major decisions or changes in lifestyle. Muriel Donnelly has received troubling, possibly fatal, news about her health. Sonny wishes to marry Sunaina (Tina Desai) but is opposed by his mother, Mrs Kapoor (Lillete Dubey) who is, in turn, being courted by Guy Chambers, a foreigner whom she regards with suspicion. Evelyn Greenslade (Judi Dench) is being courted by Douglas Ainslie (Bill Nighy), who was recently deserted by and is now divorced from his wife. Norman Cousins (Ronald Pickup) and his partner Carol Parr (Diana Hardcastle) are cheating or attempting to cheat on each other in revenge for what each believes to be the other's infidelity. In addition, Sonny's financial problems are further complicated by his discovery that his friend Kashal (Shazad Latif), has bought the building he had intended as the site of the new hotel.

All these matters and a number of other problems involving less central characters are sorted out at the rehearsal party and wedding ceremony of Sonny and Sunaina. Guy Chambers gives up his job as inspector in order to convince Mrs Kapoor that his love for her is genuine. Evelyn agrees to be with Douglas. Norman and Carol discover that they really care for one another, agreeing to stop having or trying to have extramarital affairs. Muriel wishes Sonny well in his marriage to Sunaina. And Sonny finally agrees to enter into a partnership with Kashal to open the Second Best Exotic Marigold Hotel. The issue for all of these people is trust, precisely the question that the California businessman at the beginning has concerning his investment in the new hotel. In fact, at the end of the film, he comes to India and pays a visit to Muriel: what is clear from this encounter is that he was impressed by – even perhaps attracted to – Muriel. At least he offers his respect to her for, in his words, planting trees the shade of which she will not live to enjoy. Jean Ainslie (Penelope Wilton) is the one character betraying trust, deserting Douglas who has done nothing to deserve such treatment. Moreover, Jean has not been truthful about her new lover: eventually she confesses that she works in his office and hopes to establish a relationship with him but has no other basis for her previous assertion that he is her fiancé. By contrast, the positive side of trust is represented most overtly by Sunaina who explains to Sonny, worried that she was having an affair with Kashal, that if she is ever interested in someone else she will tell him.

With the instructive exception of Jean, everyone in the film, including Muriel, is at the end left at least with the possibility of love or respect from/with someone else, a possibility that is the result of their willingness to trust another, the very issue that is the source of the plot or, in White's terms, the principle of emplotment. In fact when Guy is asked by Sonny how he would have assessed the financial viability of the hotel had he continued as the inspector, he points out that even with all its weak points he would rate it a potentially profitable business because of the atmosphere of care and concern for its guests: in effect he would have advised the investor to trust in the trust manifest at the hotel. Similarly, Muriel's voiced letter at the end of the film expressing her apology for not being at the wedding makes clear her trust and belief in Sonny. In spite of her acid comments throughout the film, she has come to have respect and fondness for Sonny, who, as she points out, makes his mistakes but is a stalwart in times of necessity and crisis. The most pervasive trope is that of mild irony like that of the interchanges between Mrs Greenslade and Muriel, a sort of rivalry that keeps both women on their toes. In the end, knowing that Muriel is entering the final stage of her life, Mrs Greenslade lets down her guard for a moment to say, 'You know, you will be missed'. This mode of comic emplotment is made emphatic by the fact that the conclusion involves marriage, a convention of comedy, and the presence of dancing, particularly at the beginning and end of the film. This free or modern version of Indian dance is emblematic of the point Muriel makes in her final letter: instead of resistance and restraint, she advises openness to the flow and natural impetus of life, trust in yourself, in others, in life itself. As an example, she offers herself, a woman who scrubbed floors for forty years and now is the manager of a hotel in India. Life is full of unexpected promise for those willing to trust and go with the flow.

The emplotment of *The Second Best Exotic Marigold Hotel* is that the fantasy of retirement in India as a sort of extended holiday can be realised by way of trust, between managers and investors, between guests and staff. In its conclusion the film makes an imaginative leap into a realm of faith in love and trust that would be very perilous for a historian. Whatever the elements of comic emplotment used by the historian, comedy is likely to serve a very different purpose; the factual world that presents clear limits to the historian is unlikely to provide much evidence for the position presented at the end of this film. The rhetorical or, in White's terms, tropological similarities between art and history do not prevent either from going their separate ways. However blurred the lines between fiction and history, this film steps over the line at the end, entering a realm of romantic comedy. Up to that final stage, the emplotment and tropes of the film could have been employed by a cultural historian writing about the life of the British retiree in India.

Emplotment in House of Cards, episode 1

In contrast to the light ironic, comic emplotment of *The Second Best Exotic Marigold Hotel*, *House of Cards* is darkly satiric, moving towards tragedy. Indeed the two main characters, Senator Francis (Frank) Underwood (Kevin Spacey) and his wife Claire (Robin Wright) are reminiscent of Richard III and the Macbeths in both ambition and ruthlessness. And Frank's frequent asides to the audience are not unlike brief versions of Shakespearian soliloquies, most prominent in *Hamlet*, which is also a revenge tragedy. The episode begins with Frank dispatching a dog badly injured by a car, explaining that pain without purpose is something he will not tolerate. However, he lies to the owners of the dog, implying that there was no way of saving the poor creature. Similarly, Claire is equally cold-hearted. In her capacity as head of a charity for clean water, she does not hesitate to discharge half of her employees in order to raise the stature of her organisation to an international level providing her with a more prominent platform for her and her husband's ambitions. As she explains to her office manager, who must decide on those to be let go, 'We may be a charitable institution but that does involve charity to our employees.' Indeed, after this unfortunate underling has completed the culling process, she is then fired by Claire.

At the outset Claire plays her part as devoted wife unflinchingly. Frank, however, is informed that the president-elect has decided to revoke his promise to appoint him secretary of state. Instead, his assistant – who actually received her appointment by way of Frank's influence – explains that the president wants the senator to remain as the majority whip to help get his programme through the legislature. When Frank returns home disconsolate and 'sorry' for not having telephoned his wife, Claire responds, 'My husband does not apologise, not even to me.' In this way, she emboldens him to pursue his revenge, and when he recovers from shock at the president's betrayal with a plan that involves 'irons in the fire' she responds, 'Fire, I like.' Following this scene, Frank and his wife attend an inaugural ball where in a series of asides he introduces the audience to the major players in this tragic drama. From the president on down, Frank has little respect for any of them except as vote-getters, people who can help him rise in the government hierarchy and then be moved out of his way. From his point of view, the government is comprised of people as ambitious as he is but who are doomed to falter in the attempt to get to the top because of self-indulgence and/or underestimation of the competition, namely, himself. He concludes his asides with 'Welcome to Washington.' And here again history mingles with fiction: however unscrupulous we consider Frank to be, few of us, I believe, doubt the accuracy of his assessment of Washington. *House of Cards* begins by announcing to its audience that if you are disillusioned with the US central government, you have tuned in to the right programme.

The tragic emplotment serves to show us the life of the ambitious and powerful in the capital of the United States; the phrase 'dog eat dog' has a special aptness for this episode. Although we expect the wheel of fortune to turn on Frank and Claire, as it surely shall, the series is about the process of acquiring and manipulating power, the infighting and backbiting that occupy the gossip columnists and spin doctors. Frank's plan involves a combination of revenge for past betrayal and a path forward for the future: he shall discredit the new secretary of state, thereby taint the new president, and eventually ascend to the presidency himself. Since this series is ongoing, one can only speculate about the fate of Frank, but Episode 1 sets the seeds of his demise. Unlike Hamlet, the great Shakespearean revenger, Frank does not inspire his followers with his principles. Instead, he entraps them by playing upon their desires and needs, rather more like Rosencrantz and Guildenstern attempting to

manipulate Hamlet. The result of using people is usually to be eventually yourself used, and so we can but expect that these victims will
finally get their revenge. Two are prominent in this opening episode.
Zoe Barnes (Kate Mara) is the ambitious young journalist who
serves as the conduit for Frank's leaks to the press that bring down
his rivals. From within the legislature, Peter Russo (Corey Stoll) is
Frank's creature, a congressman threatened with the exposure of
his record of arrests for drunk driving and possession of illegal sub-
stances that would end his political career. Here we are introduced
to the inner workings of Washington. Once Frank is informed that
Peter has again been arrested for DUI he tells his trusty aide, Doug
Stamper (Michael Kelly), to get him out of jail. Since the municipal
police made the arrest, Doug contacts a municipal politician, promising to help in his campaign to be mayor in return for releasing
Peter from custody. Somewhat surprised, Peter is freed without a
hearing or even a penalty. He soon learns that the source of this
gift, Frank, expects absolute loyalty in return, adding 'and you had
better be scared'. Understandably, Peter is indeed frightened.

Power based upon fear, secrecy and subterfuge is vulnerable;
at the first suggestion that Frank is on his way down rather than
up, these used and abused people will turn on him with damaging evidence to back up their accusations. The precariousness of
Frank's political position makes clear the meaning of the title,
House of Cards. And here we see again the parting of the ways
between fiction and history. The writer of this fictive series need
only establish that the story of Frank's ascent to the presidency
is believable; the historian would probably want to establish
that such a rise to power was more than a mere possibility. The
emplotment of a history could remain the same but the threads
of the embroidered design would have to be comprised of more
facts and less probable or believable fictions. Frank is the crea-
tion of poetic licence. This episode ends with a scene that again
combines fact and fiction. Frank visits his favourite spare-rib restaurant, more accurately called a 'joint', as in 'hamburger joint',
in a rather run-down section of Washington, DC. Clearly, he is a
regular here, well known to the proprietor. Relishing two help-
ings of spare ribs early in the morning – clearly a man of strong
digestion – Frank tells us that here he feels at one with his past, a
poor boy from South Carolina who worked his way up the hard
way. We are being shown the seat of Frank's ambition, an appetite

for power that began in a world neglected by power, a place of no interest to Washington power-brokers, a place no doubt of such poverty and despair that few there even bother to vote. Frank's overweening appetite, his passion for power, stems from contempt of Washington, an opinion that is, I believe, shared by a majority of the electorate of the United States. So the story of *House of Cards* is fictive, but it is based upon fact, one axiom of present-day politics in the United States being that any candidate demonstrating that they are not a part of the political establishment has a distinct advantage. If nothing else, the meteoric rise of Donald Trump exemplifies that point. The success of this series rests upon the assumption of general disrespect for Washington politics and its participants, an assumption that however prevalent is an interpretation, not a fact. It lends historical credibility to the fictional story of Frank and Claire Underwood. Historians may question the accuracy of this view of Washington, but they will then be obliged to provide an alternative interpretation of US establishment politics, not merely facts, to underpin their revised historical narrative.

Tropology and culture: Jennifer Lee and Chris Buck's *Frozen* (2013) and Jonathan Teplitzky's *The Railway Man* (2013)

White explains what he means by tropology as follows:

> Tropology is not, of course, a theory of language, but more or less a systemized cluster of notions about figurative language deriving from neo-classical rhetorics. It thus provides a perspective on language from which to analyze the elements, levels, and combinational procedures of non-formalized and especially pragmatic discourses. Tropology centres attention on the 'turns' in a discourse, turns from one level of generalization to another, from a description to an analysis or the reverse, from a figure to a ground or from an event to its context, from the conventions of one genre to another in one discourse (Cohen, *Future* 28).

These movements in a discourse of what might be called structural styles – referred to as metaphor, metonymy, synecdoche, and irony – are further defined using Northrop Frye's literary categories:

The tropological structures of metaphor, metonymy, synecdoche, and irony (and what I take – following Northrop Frye – to be their corresponding plot types: Romance, Comedy, Tragedy, and Satire), provide us with a much more refined classification of the kinds of historical discourses than that based on the distinction between 'linear' and 'cyclical' representations of historical processes. They also allow us to see more clearly the ways in which historical discourse resembles and indeed converges with fictional narrative, both in the strategies it uses to endow events with meanings and in the kinds of truth in which it deals (Cohen, *Future* 29).

These tropological turns are, according to White, of cultural significance:

Tropology is especially useful for the analysis of narrative historiography, because narrative history is a mode of discourse in which the relations between what a given culture regards as literal truths and figurative truths expressed in its characteristic fictions, the kinds of stories it tells about itself and about others, can be tested. In historical narrative, the dominant plot forms used by a culture to 'imagine' the different kinds of meaning (tragic, comic epic, farcical etc.) that a distinctively human form of life *might have* are tested against the information and knowledge that specific forms of life *have had* in the past. In the process, not only are human forms of past life endowed with the kinds of meaning met with in the forms of fiction produced by a given culture, but the degrees of 'truthfulness' and 'realism' of these forms of fiction to the facts of historical reality and our knowledge of it can be measured (Cohen, *Future* 36).

Tropology in Frozen

Animated films often make tropology more overt. *Frozen*, for example, moves frequently and with apparent ease between extremes of winter and summer, indicative of tropological turns from comedy to tragedy. Princess Elsa, soon to be queen, is born with the capacity to turn ice into water and vice versa. She soon becomes aware of the perils to others of her powers but not until the end of the film does she discover the antidote, namely love and concern for another. Her freezing powers first become apparent at an early age when she inadvertently harms her beloved sister Anna. Alarmed, her parents, the king and queen of Arendelle, isolate her from her beloved sister, hoping to teach her to control and conceal her powers. The two sisters become alienated from one another, neither understanding the chasm of difference that has suddenly separated them. Upon unexpectedly becoming queen, Elsa must appear in public and once again risk harming those whom she loves, leading to her decision to retreat to a private ice kingdom in the north to avoid all human contact. Eventually, she discovers her ability to thaw her frozen victims as well as her own lonely heart by expressing her natural love.

This theme is expressed vividly by way of visual scenes, palaces and entire kingdoms of ice set in winter landscapes that constitute forms of ice sculpture, and by way of music: most of the dialogue is in the form of song or recitative. By this means the fantasy element is accentuated, particularly when Elsa is able suddenly to transform an entire landscape from summer into winter, or miraculously freeze an entire fjord, escaping over the ice from her enemy. These turns represent the deep inner feelings of a young, vulnerable woman trying to come to terms with her largely unconscious emotions. The allegory here is of psychological maturation, in particular the realisation that repression or denial is to be distinguished from control, that is, the channelling of feelings to serve good purposes, as, in the end, when Elsa's power serves to save her beloved sister's life.

At the same time that this fictional or fantasy story is unfolding, there is, as White suggests, a cultural or historical tale of daily life in the kingdom. The coronation of Queen Elsa gladdens Anna's heart but provides access to the kingdom for nefarious elements, in particular the Duke of Weselton who comes, as he freely admits, to 'exploit' the kingdom. In this way, the twists and turns of the courtship of the young princesses are bound up with the social and political life of the realm. Most important in this regard is the fact that the evil courtier, Hans, is an outsider, in contrast to Kristoff the virtuous lover, an indigenous inhabitant. Interestingly, Kristoff, a commoner, again in contrast to Hans who is an aristocrat, is by profession an iceman, one who cuts the ice to sell to the inhabitants for preserving food.

Kristoff serves his princess, Anna, by leading her to the mountain ice kingdom in her quest for Elsa. He then helps her literally break through the ice palace to rescue the queen from the Duke of Weselton's thugs, who are attempting to kill her. Elsa, however, remains reticent about returning from the north because she continues to be unaware of her ability to save her ice victims by way of love. Only when Anna appears to die in her effort to save Elsa from the clutches of Hans does she by way of mourning for her sister discover her ability to revive her ice victims. In short, love is first experienced as coming from another. The film demonstrates that these sheltered young women first discover love by responding to others' love for them, a concept that could be described as an element of psychological reality in this fantasy film.

The historical element of this fantasy film is transformed by the young women's discovery of the power of love. The movie ends with the removal of the baddies, Hans in chains, and the duke banished back to his native land. The sisters become again great friends, and Queen Elsa rewards her loyal followers and exiles the enemies of Arendelle. The interchange here between fiction/fantasy and cultural history is instructive. Fantasy enables sheltered and repressed young women to discover their passions, particularly the power of love. This discovery has historical application, restoring peace and stability to the realm. The tropology of ice/water, winter/summer applies to the psyches of the young women and to the socio-political state of the kingdom.

Tropology and culture in The Railway Man

In contrast to the fantasy element of *Frozen*, *The Railway Man* is, as we are informed at the outset, 'a true story'. In fact, the film derives from an autobiography of the main character, Eric Lomax (Colin Firth), who was still alive when the film was being made: Colin Firth, who met Eric Lomax in Berwick-upon-Tweed where part of the film is set, is reported to have said the following:

> I think what is not often addressed is the effect over time. We do sometimes see stories about what it's like coming home from war, we very rarely see stories about what it's like decades later. This is not just a portrait of suffering. It's about relationships ... how that damage interacts with intimate relationships, with love (*The Guardian*, 24 June 2015, p. 12).

The tropology pursued in this film is that of a man whose wartime wounds lead to his closing down, turning inward, allowing his original enthusiasm for trains to become an obsession, a substitute for society. Not surprisingly, he meets his wife Patti (Nicole Kidman) on a train. With clever empathy, Patti encourages the withdrawn Eric to speak about trains. He falls in love because her beauty is intimately bound up with her capacity to open herself to the pain of others – a nurse by profession and natural inclination. With the exception of those who may have read the autobiography that provided the basis for the film, the audience cannot determine the historical accuracy of the account of Eric and Patti's courtship and love relationship; we accept it as a convenient fiction serving the story of a man and woman who together share the aftermath of a war, a particularly terrible tale of heroism and torture.

After seeing what Eric underwent in a Japanese war prison, we understand his peculiar behaviour, even his neglect of and occasional coldness to his loving wife. When his friend and fellow prisoner Finlay (Stellan Skarsgård) shows him a newspaper clipping of the interpreter who was present throughout his torture and is still alive, the question of how Eric will come to terms with his past becomes palpable. Finlay gives him a Japanese dagger and asks him – actually begs him – to avenge the cruelty of their Japanese captors. Shortly thereafter, Finlay hangs himself; when Patti remarks that she feared Eric would imitate his action, he replies, 'Finlay was different; he did not have you.' And here we confront what Colin Firth refers to in the quotation above, not merely the effect of the war but the effect over time that is complicated by subsequent love.

The vivid re-enactment of the daily life of the prisoners in itself makes the desire for revenge more than understandable. The torture of Eric is particularly savage and utterly futile. They discover the hidden radio receiver and want to know what he was intending to transmit. When he points out repeatedly that the machine is not capable of send-ing any signal, they accuse him of lying. Finally after repeatedly being mercilessly tortured he tells them why he wanted a receiver: it raises the morale of the prisoners to hear that Allied forces are gradually winning the war, as he puts it, destroying your cities, homes, and families. Again, they accuse him of lying and continue with brutality, astonished that he survives. With this ordeal fresh in our minds, we more than under-stand when Eric approaches the Japanese interpreter, Takashi Nagase (Hiroyuki Sanada), intending to wreak his revenge. But he finds Nagase attempting to achieve reconciliation with his old enemies.

Instead of pursuing revenge, he sets about schooling Nagase in remorse. When Nagase refers to the killing of prisoners, Eric amends the word to *murder* and makes Nagase repeat it. When Nagase insists that he was just an interpreter not a member of the army, Eric counters that he witnessed every atrocity carried out by the army. By this means, Eric allays some of his deep anger and frees himself of some of the ghosts of his past. Eric also recapitulates with Nagase the various stages of his imprisonment, even torturing him by threatening to kill him, making him feel, as had Eric often on the torture table, that he was about to die.

The details of Eric's torture and those of Nagase occupy a good portion of this gruelling film, and they do have a historical/artistic function. The torture of Eric is particularly ghastly because they at first believe him to be a spy. When he finally confesses that his only reason for the radio was to raise the morale of the prisoners to help them believe that the Allies were winning the war and that their ordeal would some day, if they survived, end, the Japanese nonetheless continue the torture. Nagase explains that they did not believe Eric's account of how the war was going against them, certainly not that their homes and families were being destroyed while they continued serving their country. After all, to believe him would be, in effect, to make themselves his prisoner, a frighteningly unthinkable possibility. And when Eric becomes the torturer, he experiences something similar. At the beginning, he treats Nagase as his prisoner, even placing him in the kneeling cage that he had once occupied. He is unable to carry on with the procedure because, unlike his Japanese captors during the war, he has an alternative life with Patti. The only alternative available to the Japanese during the war would have been acceptance of what Eric told them, that is, the imminence of defeat and the expectation that they would then be treated as they have treated their prisoners of war. History, as in the progression from then, during the war, to now, after the war, has altered the situation for both Eric and Nagase. And the concept of the historical progression of torture is the subject of this film, a historical insight about history as change. And while we are in no position to know how factual the details of this film are, few, I expect, would contest this point about how history changes the nature of torture, fiction again in the service of history.

The final stage comes after Eric returns home to Patti. Now with renewed appreciation for her patient and persistent love, he receives a letter from Nagase admitting that he was in the Japanese army. During their confrontation he had claimed that he was only a translator, not a soldier. Now he completes his confession, owning up to being an integral part of the group that tortured him so severely. Eric asks Patti to accompany him back to confront Nagase. The very moving final scene of forgiveness involves Eric and Patti as well as a truly remorseful Nagase. Now we recall Finlay telling Patti of Eric's act of incredible heroism in taking full responsibility for the transmitter that had in fact been a joint venture among the prisoners and laying down his spectacles as an act of submission. We now recognise that Eric's act of forgiveness results not only from Nagase's full confession and Patti's unconditional love but also from Eric's strength of inner being, indicated by his earlier relinquishing his spectacles to his captors and now by his refusal to take revenge.

The conclusion relies on the exceptional nature of the three main characters, Nagase's heartfelt regret, Patti's ceaseless love, and Eric's courageous belief in reconciliation. The historian is likely to argue that the possibility of these three types of characters coming together in an actual event is remote and, if it did happen, singular in nature. The fictionalist is not troubled by the improbability or the singularity: his point is rather to delineate the necessary human ingredients for the process of reconciliation. Both gain from the interchange. Even imagining a factional or other sort of blurred generic narrative, the writer could maintain that the possibility, however remote and singular, remains a possibility and is therefore not necessarily ahistorical. However, the cultural historian can point to the fact that the Japanese prison guards must learn how to confess, to own up to crime, and that the prisoners must come to relinquish hate and its familiar partner, despair. *Frozen* and *The Railway Man* occupy opposite poles in the continuum from fiction to history. The fantasy of *Frozen* serves to thaw the cold realm of repressed female psyches, and *The Railway Man* at least gives grounds for hope of reconciliation. White's point is that the two disciplines are related, making use of similar tropological devices but for different purposes. A very different consideration might involve a narrative from Patti's point of view; my next chapter explores the female perspective and the tropological characteristics of women's language.

3 Julia Kristeva: the female perspective on culture

Kristeva takes literary interpretation for granted: her argument is that the female point of view must be included into the interpretive perspective. She sees three stages of feminism. In the first section, I examine Mad Men *and* Spooks *to show the first stage of feminism. Women have achieved certain legal rights and equality in the workplace, but these television programmes show that, as Kristeva predicted, this advancement does not mean that the feminine interpretive perspective is accepted by the male establishment. In the second phase, women develop a language of their own because treated as mute by the male world.* The Iron Lady *and* Spanglish *illustrate feminine language. In the final section, the ideal, a combination of male and female within what Kristeva calls the 'nuclei' of men and women is seen in* Philomena *and* The Hundred-Foot Journey.

Born in Bulgaria in 1941, Julia Kristeva, Professor at the University of Paris, Diderot, moved to Paris when she was twenty-four years old and received her advanced training there. In addition to her academic position, she is a practising psychoanalyst. While she has written many books and essays, I shall focus on what is perhaps her most important and influential assessment of the cultural situation of women, entitled 'Women's Time', first published in 1979 as 'Le Temps des femmes'.

This essay begins by establishing a basic distinction between male and female time. For Kristeva, men think of time in linear terms, that is, in relation to production, what can be done or accomplished in a limited period of chronological time. Women, on the other hand, are more likely to consider time not in terms of production but of reproduction, 'survival of the species, life and death, the body, sex, and symbol' (Kristeva, 189). 'In other words, we confront two temporal dimensions: (for men) the time of linear history or *cursive time* (as Nietzsche called it) and (for women) the time of another history, thus another time, *monumental time* (again according to Nietzsche) which englobes these supra-national socio-cultural ensembles within even larger entities' (Kristeva 189). The goal of Kristeva's essay is to suggest – hope is probably more accurate – that males and females can combine these two mental dispositions in a way of thinking that is no longer divided in sexist terms. Kristeva describes two 'generations' of feminism preparing the way for the present or third generation where fusion of the male and female first begins but is still developing.

Phase one: the socio-political battle – Matthew Weiner's *Mad Men*, series 6, episode 1 (2013) and David Wolstencroft's *Spooks*, series 10, episode 3 (2011)

Kristeva operates on the assumption that the relationship between men and women is key to understanding and improving the psycho-social world of our daily lives. Women, according to Kristeva, entered into the socio-political arena not by way of ideology but as the result of the '*logic of identification*', that is, with certain 'logical and ontological values of a rationality dominant in the nation-state' (194). Kristeva explains that the first women's movement, 'the struggle of suffragists and of existential feminists ... while immediately universalist [in scope was] also deeply rooted in the socio-political life of nations' (193). The initial struggles and accomplishments of feminism are at once universal, having significance for all women, and historical, pertaining to particular problems in different nations. In what she calls 'phase one', by means of solidarity women established the following rights: 'abortion, contraception, equal pay, professional recognition' (194). Of course, Kristeva is not arguing that these rights have been fully accomplished, only that they have been established in the eyes of most people in power as worthy and ultimately possible. The struggle for realisation continues but for the most part is only deterred by practical and temporary problems. Those opposed in principle to these rights are considered extreme and usually marginalised. And the implication is that aside from this continuing practical struggle women have moved to a different theoretical level or phase two, to be considered in detail in the next section. Briefly, if phase one is a demand for equality with men then phase two is an assertion of difference, specifically that represented by a female language.

Phase one and Mad Men, series 6, episode 1

As the title *Mad Men* suggests, this television series takes place in the male-dominated Madison Avenue advertising world of the 1960s: here we would expect to see Kristeva's phase one in the making. I shall focus on the dilemma of the two main female characters, Peggy (Elisabeth Moss) and Joan (Christina Hendricks). Peggy, the less attractive of the two but higher up in the firm at this point, is erratic and puzzling in her behaviour. In the opening scene, Freddy does his 'schtick' on a campaign for Accutron watches. Peggy compliments him for hitting a home run but then adds how surprised she is. Crestfallen, Freddy responds that she could have found a nicer way of saying that she had not expected much of him. In short, Peggy's backhanded compliment exposes her strategy; promotion of her own alternative slogan that she believes will in the long run prove superior to Freddy's. By contrast, Freddy simply wants to win this particular round of the competition, convincing the client to go ahead with the ad according to his presentation. Peggy, however, is thinking in more 'monumental' terms, namely, how to keep the account not just now but for the future: if Freddy's jingle is adopted but then is not successful in attracting more business for Accutron, the advertising company may in the future lose the account. Peggy believes that while Freddy's phrase may win the day, convincing the executives of the watch company to go ahead with the ad, her motto will ultimately sell more watches, gaining Accutron a larger share of the market in the long term. Her male superiors do not understand Peggy's strategy. Freddy thinks she is competing with him for the best motto. And their superior is so puzzled by Peggy's continuing to go on about a matter he considers settled that he finally says to her, 'I don't know, Peggy, I guess I am just immune to your charms', making clear that he thinks Peggy is merely making a play for him, not really concerned about the watch advertisement.

Joan faces a similar problem. Sent by her immediate superior to meet an account executive considered beneath him in the corporate hierarchy, Joan discovers that the executive plans to start advertising in-house, resulting in the loss of a large account for the firm. Cleverly, Joan uses her female charm and quick intelligence to convince the man in charge to postpone his final decision, giving her

boss time to make a counter-offer. Distracted with another nego-
tiation her boss does not recognise the emergency, leaving town
to attend to another problem. Bravely taking the matter into her
own hands, Joan telephones the account executive from her boss's
office. Speaking with the forcefulness of a top manager, she points
out to this young, inexperienced business-school graduate – and,
importantly, she herself has no such academic credentials – that his
business will be competing with them in their world, not his, where
they have long-term connections and thirty other accounts while he
will have neither. In this way, she saves the account. When her boss
returns, instead of congratulating her for her brilliant performance
under pressure, he thanks her perfunctorily, throws her earring at
her, warning her never to use his office again. While Joan is thinking
in larger or 'monumental' terms of saving the account for the future,
her boss simply thinks she is muscling in on his territory: he is fighting a battle while she is trying to win the war.

Not surprisingly, the men with power in this episode and indeed
throughout the series have troubled relationships with women. Don
Draper (Jon Hamm) is divorced and involved with a woman in
California, a relationship that is clearly not working. The problem
involves his girlfriend's attempt to break into show business as an
actress. She needs and wants to be in Los Angeles while Don prefers to do his business from New York City. The resulting bicoastal
liaison is unsatisfactory. Although Don tolerates his partner's career
ambition, showing an understanding of the new, emancipated
woman in contrast to his own ex-wife, a traditional stay-at-home
mother of their three children, he is unable to change his own way
of life to make the new relationship viable. His firm does have an
office in Los Angeles, but he insists on staying in New York City.
Similarly, Roger Sterling (John Slattery), the partner who hired Don
and his closest colleague, also has unsuccessful relationships with
women. Divorced, Roger lives with a woman who has an open bed
where he finds himself on occasion with two women or two men
and probably, we imagine, other combinations. When his daughter
invites him to brunch he assumes that her purpose is to ask for
money and is taken aback when she explains that the invitation
was to provide an opportunity to forgive him for making her ask
him for money and for the messy divorce from her mother. Clearly,
the daughter has outmanoeuvred her stunned father; she has the
measure of him, and he does not know what to make of it. Like

Don's girlfriend, Sterling's daughter has achieved the level of emancipation of phase one. These women refuse to accept the control of men, either as fathers or lovers, but it is not clear how this new freedom will change the men or their attitudes towards women. Nor is it clear what the women can achieve by way of this new freedom. Peggy is lonely and frustrated. Joan is angry with Don for not pulling his weight at work but can do little about it. And we cannot but wonder if Sterling's daughter will once again have to ask her father for money. This cultural stage for women is a very precarious one. This episode of *Mad Men*, unlike Kristeva, does not offer much hope that these independent women will be able to change or even influence the male establishment.

Phase one and Spooks, series 10, episode 3

The next generation is not quite what Kristeva predicted. The third episode of *Spooks*, series 10, illustrates the dilemma of women still in phase one but at a later date since the action of this series is, unlike the 1960s of *Mad Men*, contemporary, that is, from 2002 to 2011. And of course, MI5, a bastion of male machismo, is bound to be well behind the society at large with regard to the advances of feminism. The key moment, in my view, is the lunchtime conversation between Ruth (Nicola Walker) and the home secretary (Robert Glenister), who is trying to pry her loose from her attachment to her immediate superior, Harry (Peter Firth), the head of MI5. In a rare moment of candour no doubt encouraged by the wine, Ruth admits that although it sounds strange coming from someone in the field of espionage she is tired of secrets because they keep you from knowing people. Here is a vivid example of the sort of monumental or reproductive time that Kristeva mentions in contrast to Harry and the home secretary who pursue linear goals in their professional and personal lives. Indeed, the home secretary misunderstands Ruth; he offers her career advancement, part of his calculated and very linear attempt to seduce her. Not surprisingly, nothing further happens between them; the home secretary's narrow focus upon ambition and sex indicates that he has completely misunderstood Ruth's point of view. What she was expressing to this ambitious careerist is that the spooks' world is a lonely one where people cannot afford to give their hearts to others. The home secretary's offer of a new position at a desk and in bed is even more impersonal than what she experiences at MI5.

And the episode itself demonstrates the chasm between males and females in a world that does not in principle oppose the concept of sexual equality since *Spooks*, we again need to keep in mind, is set in the present when most people presumably accept the new rights of women achieved in phase one. Now matters are more complicated. The MI5 office, although full of women, is dominated by the men, Harry, the boss, and his agent Dimitri (Max Brown). They in turn are opposed by two dominant men, the Russian diplomat and his son.

The story involves a double plot; the main plot concerns an anarchist bomb threat and the subplot an investigation into the recent death of an MI5 agent. In both plots women play an important role but usually remain in the background. The anarchist villain is approached by way of his sister in what is characterised as a 'honey pot' strategy; Dimitri, a handsome young MI5 agent, poses as Ryan, an internet date, to gain the trust of the innocent sister. Because the anarchist is believed to be armed with a 'dirty bomb', that is, a nuclear device, he takes precedence over the murder investigation of the MI5 agent that is relegated to the subplot. Nonetheless, Harry encourages his agents to continue surreptitiously their search for the murderer of their colleague. To further this investigation he sends Ruth as his representative to Elena, the wife of the senior Russian diplomat. The resulting conversation is another example of a distinctly feminine perspective. Elena meets Ruth at the National Gallery in front of the picture *The Execution of Lady Jane Grey*. Since Jane Grey was queen for nine days before being executed by Queen Mary we have two women gazing at the result of the conflict between two queens of England. The conversation between the women in this scene is not combative. Elena asks Ruth if Harry loves her. Ruth replies that she has no idea how to answer that question. Then Elena asks if Harry trusts her, to which Ruth murmurs 'not always', provoking Elena to remark that Harry's job prevents him from completely trusting anyone all of the time, including himself. We see here how differently the women view the world and their time in it from the men. Harry has sent Ruth to inquire about the murder of their colleague, but Elena and Ruth talk about Harry since each has or did have a personal relationship with him. For the women, the larger question of Harry's affection and loyalty takes precedence over the murder investigation, since they both realise that after the murder is sorted out, if it ever is, their relation with

Harry may affect the rest of their lives. The picture in the background suggests that both women, like Lady Jane Grey and Queen Mary, will not prevail in power for long in a patriarchal society.

Although Ruth and Elena are permitted to express their views freely, they cannot remain uncontaminated – to use an appropriate nuclear term – by the male perspective. Elena, as a double spy, has been implicated in the death of a friend of her son, as has Harry, Elena's minder and the father of her son. Ruth, too, is contaminated by Harry's view of time. In the final episode while Ruth takes the 'bullet' intended for Harry, Elena turns out to be using her double-spy status to bolster the male establishment of her native country; she is really a Russian agent posing as a double spy. Although tolerating the females, the males dominate or at least their view of the world prevails over that of the females. However, the conclusion makes clear how the feminine position differs from that of the men, most emphatically when the female agent who pressed her male counterpart to enter into the honey-pot scheme with what they both believe is an innocent woman writes a letter on his behalf breaking off the relationship. She explains that the letter composed for him is what she would have wanted to receive in a similar situation. The implication is that as a man he is not capable of writing an appropriate letter, an implication borne out by the fact that, unable to bring himself to speak on the phone to the sister, he posts the letter written by his female colleague.

The subplot is not resolved until later in the series when we learn that Elena had used the pretence of being a double spy to trap Harry into giving her vital information that eventually led to the death of the MI5 agent. In fact, Elena is such a fanatic that she willingly risked the life of her son to further the Russian cause. *Spooks* then shows us two sides of women, the innocent sister and the fanatical mother. Elena's fanaticism results in her being strangled to death by her husband. Her pose as the innocent woman victim – she explains to Harry and her son that her decision to be a Russian spy was in order to achieve revenge for the assassination of her parents by the KGB – is revealed as a lie exposing her to the detestation of even those on her side. Although a Russian diplomat, her husband cannot abide a woman who would sacrifice her own son for 'Mother Russia'. For Kristeva, Elena remains at phase one trying unsuccessfully to imitate men, a sort of machismo mother. In the end she is at a loss for words to defend herself; that is why Kristeva characterises the next stage as women's language. Both *Mad Men* and *Spooks* show women caught in their own web, attempting unsuccessfully to imitate men. While Kristeva views phase one as just that, a phase or part of a unfolding process, *Mad Men* and *Spooks* show us women and men who are caught in the web of phase one, trapped by this first stage of feminist freedom. The men are incapable of understanding the new women, and the women are confined for the most part to imitating the ways of the men. Phase two requires an insistence on an alternative to female machismo.

Phase two: the language of women in Phyllida Lloyd's *The Iron Lady* (2011) and James L. Brooks' *Spanglish* (2004)

Kristeva explains that the second generation of feminists, who came to the fore after the May 1968 uprising in France but soon became international in scope, are disillusioned with the political sphere and seek an alternative to male language as a means of radically altering the feminist project. This group of women, 'qualitatively different from the first one ... seek to give a language to the intra-subjective and corporeal experiences left mute by culture in the past' (Kristeva, 194). Demanding recognition of an 'irreducible identity without equal in the opposite sex ... this feminism situates itself outside the linear time of identities which communicate through projection and revindication' (Kristeva, 194). By this means – like the first generation but with a different strategy, one involving language – these feminists move from linear, male time to monumental or female time.

Phase two and The Iron Lady
A portrait of Margaret Thatcher in retirement, *The Iron Lady* may seem an odd choice to exemplify disillusionment with the political world, but the film, in my view, proceeds by way of a feminine voice – namely Margaret Thatcher's inner dialogue with her late husband Denis (Jim Broadbent) – showing the first female prime minister of Great Britain, in spite of her political achievements, struggling to find a female language. While the film makes reference to the major political high and low points of Thatcher's career as leader of the Conservative Party and her eleven and a half years as

prime minister, the storyline or narrative voice is almost exclusively in the form of imaginary conversations with her husband, Denis, who we know from the beginning of the film to be dead. Moreover, the movie begins with Thatcher (Meryl Streep) alone in retirement and rather doddery, buying a bottle of milk and a newspaper in a local shop without being recognised; the film concludes with her alone in the kitchen washing up a teacup, something she vowed never to do when Denis proposed marriage.

One result of this continual imaginary domestic conversation between husband and wife is that in the film family takes precedence over politics, the very opposite of her public persona. Thatcher always appeared in real life to prioritise her political position over her personal domestic responsibilities. The film, by contrast, takes the public persona for granted as already well known in order to focus on her private life after retirement. She and Denis have their ups and downs, particularly when he points to her overweening political ambition that makes family secondary. Indeed, at one point he suggests that the political changes she has instituted may well not survive history. Her relationship with her daughter seems to be one of duty more than love. The one happy moment between mother and daughter is when Margaret is teaching Carol to drive. Her daughter soon awakens from the illusion that for a brief period she has been the centre of her mother's attention when Margaret announces that she has decided during the drive to run for head of the Conservative Party. Carol (Olivia Colman) leaves in a huff, and Denis, in a rare moment of uncontrollable temper, remarks, 'Margaret you are insufferable'. Her son Mark never appears in the film except to explain on the phone that he cannot come to the unveiling of her portrait at the Houses of Parliament. When she attempts to excuse him by pointing out that bringing the family from South Africa is very expensive, Denis remarks that she is forever making excuses for their ne'er-do-well son. Although Carol visits her mother regularly and shows real concern for her, their relationship is unsatisfactory for both. Carol tries to offer affection and care but is told that she fusses too much. Instead, Margaret encourages her daughter to follow her own example as a young woman, occupying her mind with ideas rather than fussing over her mother. Somewhat bewildered, Carol must think that is precisely the reason why her mother has always been so distant from her children.

While her role as mother and wife is often perfunctory and unsuccessful, she is nonetheless portrayed as a brilliant and charismatic politician, the first female and longest-serving prime minister of the twentieth century. In retirement her public achievements bring her only momentary pleasure, particularly as she always hears her inner voice, that of Denis, suggesting that her greatest achievements, the victory in the Falklands War or the defeat of the coal miners' union, may be ephemeral. A key moment in the film is when Denis, stumped by a crossword puzzle clue, asks Margaret for help, knowing, as he puts it, that she will get it. And so she does. The answer is 'obstinate', an element deeply imbued in her personality since her youth. The saddest instance of this trait and most damaging to her career is with Geoffrey Howe (Anthony Head), her loyal follower, who, when he has the temerity to disagree with her, is publicly humiliated so viciously that, as one fellow Tory puts it, no decent person would treat his gamekeeper in such a way. And Howe's resignation speech in Parliament is the beginning of the end for Margaret. Here the turning point is marked by a change in her language. At the cabinet meeting, she humiliates Howe, speaking and behaving like a schoolmistress scolding him for his misspelling, crossly snapping her fingers, insisting on using his pencil to correct his mistakes. He must feel like an unruly child sitting on the naughty step. At this crucial moment when her own party is turning against her she goes abroad to a meeting, leaving them to their machinations, returning to face defeat and finally her reluctant resignation. Prior to this point, Thatcher's public performance was always a polished combination of male and female language, clear and assertive but never aggressive or angry. Her downfall occurs when the headiness of power leads her to use the language and gestures of an irritated housewife.

Yet Meryl Streep's portrayal, which resulted in her nomination for an Academy Award, shows that Margaret was capable of love, certainly for Denis and also for her children. We see her deep concern for her family in the 'inner' or imaginary conversations of Margaret and Denis, a technique that is two-sided. It exposes a different element of Thatcher's personality but also shows that she cannot express her love in the language of politics that dominates her life until retirement. Indeed, the scene of voice lessons is very telling in this regard. She is given exercises in lowering her voice to suggest authority, that is, to sound more like a man. And ironically she uses female body language while practising, as if a part of her has become what Kristeva calls 'mute'. In fact, Margaret has always been mentored by men. As a young girl working in her father's grocery shop, hearing his speeches during his campaign for mayor of Grantham, she first becomes indoctrinated by the concept of being self-reliant rather than dependent on state welfare. The Tory ministers and advisers who change her voice and manner of dressing are only giving a new appearance to old male Tory views that derive from her father. At the end of the film, finally accepting that Denis is gone for ever, Margaret panics for a moment, but then she hears him saying, as he has many times in the past, 'You will be all right on your own, you always have been.' Is he suggesting that she will be all right on her own now that he is gone or that she has always been on her own, or perhaps both? Denis suggests that Margaret's female side has remained mute; she succeeded in politics by internalising the language of men – from her father to Airey Neave and Geoffrey Howe – in a female voice without any shrillness. Sadly, she ends alone, unable to express her love for her family. And we are left with an understanding of why Kristeva insists that this next stage must involve not merely the voice but also the language of women.

Phase two and Spanglish

Spanglish portrays a more successful attempt at communicating by way of a female language. The title refers most obviously to the linguistic struggle of the protagonist, a Mexican mother (Paz Vega) who emigrates to the USA without any English; she attempts to use the language of her new country by way of what is aptly termed Spanglish. In addition, her young daughter, Cristina (Aimee Garcia) who almost immediately speaks English like a native, is caught between languages because until her mother masters the new tongue Cristina is involved in constant simultaneous translation. The daughter also employs a version of Spanglish that is particularly feminine since she is for the most part rendering in English the gestures and body language as well as the Spanish words of her mother.

The movie begins and ends with the reading of an essay by Cristina, telling the story of the film as part of her application to Princeton University. The film is a dramatic presentation of her letter, showing that female language is bound up with female behaviour. Cristina remembers her father leaving the family when she was six, still living in Mexico. A sensitive, bright child, she realises that her mother tries to hide her despair from her daughter, never allowing Cristina to see her crying. But Cristina hears her sobbing. When Cristina is twelve years old, Flor, her mother, takes her across the border from Mexico into the United States, where as a single mother as well as an immigrant she plans to raise and educate her daughter. Now aged eighteen, Cristina is eligible to apply for university. The film that ensues is the story of how she developed to this high linguistic and academic level, a narrative derived from and based upon her language. In fact, at times the film features Cristina's language. A good example occurs when, upon first seeing the luxurious homes on Malibu beach, she remarks that never before had she seen houses with oceans as their backyard.

Cristina's language functions not merely to present a poor Mexican girl's view of upper-middle-class California but as part of her attempt to convince the admissions committee at Princeton to admit her and offer her a scholarship. We as viewers of the film join with the admissions committee, judging whether Cristina deserves a scholarship to this prestigious university. And seeing admissions committee members tossing aside boring essays, we realise that language is crucial to Cristina's future and is the basis of the film's ability to hold audience interest.

Cristina's essay and the film focus on her mother, not merely on her struggle to survive and to provide for her daughter but on a crucial decision made at the end of the film. Flor works as a housekeeper for the Clasky family in an upper-middle-class suburb of Los Angeles. At first she commutes from her apartment to her job, but for summer vacation Mrs Clasky, Deb (Téa Leoni) rents a beach home, inviting Flor and her daughter to join them. Both of the Claskys take to Cristina, who is bright, appreciative, and adept at simultaneous translation, facilitating communication between the Claskys and her mother. Eventually Deb helps Cristina get a scholarship at the posh private school that her daughter Bernice (Sarah Steele) attends, and Mr Clasky (Adam Sandler) is generous and kind to Flor and her daughter. Gradually, Flor begins to believe that Cristina is slipping away from her, becoming an upper-middle-class American. In the end, she quits the job and takes Cristina away from the privileged private school, asking her, 'Is what you want for yourself, to become very different from me?' As they ride away in the bus from the Claskys, Cristina snuggles up to her mother. The answer to her mother's question is the essay itself that concludes by declaring, 'Everything I am I owe to my mother.'

Flor's decision to take her daughter away from the privileged existence of the Claskys is based upon what she sees while living with them. John is a loving husband and devoted father: his biggest problem derives paradoxically from his success as a chef. His restaurant, having received a rave review, is no longer available to the regular walk-in neighbourhood clients. He feels the restaurant has lost its heart and now involves his having to be at work at times that he wishes to spend with his family. While he manages to cope with these problems, his wife and mother-in-law have more serious difficulties. His mother-in-law, although kind and gentle, is on her way to becoming an alcoholic. His wife, Deb, made redundant and now deeply dissatisfied with being a stay-at-home housewife, has an affair with a real-estate agent. In addition, Deb and John have different views about how to treat their daughter, Bernice, a sweet and loving child of about twelve years old who is overweight. Deb wants her to lose weight, but John feels that it is more important to focus on her schoolwork than on physical appearance. What becomes clear to Flor is that John has the sensibility of a woman like herself, being more capable of empathy and tolerance than his wife. At first Flor thinks that John lacks the machismo of a proper man, but she soon comes to admire his forbearance and steadfastness. And here it is important to recognise that Cristina is particularly adept at translating John's English for her mother because he often uses female language. Kristeva would, I believe, point out that female language is not exclusive to women but an alternative available to everyone.

In fact, Flor comes to understand that John is not a typical male: she admires his ability to empathise with others, to put his concern and care for others above his own needs. Flor is further drawn to John because she sees that he is taken for granted by his wife, another crucial element of the plot revealed by way of female language. When Deb is riding in the convertible of the man who will become her lover, she is unable to control her hair in the wind. The cool, handsome driver suggests, as we imagine he has with many others, that she move her seat forward. Marvelling at how her hair is now swept backward, as in a Hollywood film, Deb remarks, 'You must be trouble', and he is. By contrast, the turning point between Flor and John – again a female-language moment – is when Flor is angry at John for giving Cristina a large amount of money earned by collecting stones on the beach. She regards this gift as interference, the implication being that it is far more money than she could ever afford to give to her daughter. In a rare moment of defensive anger, one that is female and linguistic, not male and physical, John calls Flor a hypocrite because she had interfered in their upbringing of Bernice by altering the overtight clothes bought for her by her mother to encourage her to diet. Flor immediately climbs down, apologising, and John is taken aback at this sudden reversal. He comes to see that Flor is decent and fair-minded, beginning to fall in love with her. Interestingly, it is at this point that Flor declares that she must learn English; she needs to speak to John in her own right, not by way of her daughter's translation. Later, after having learned English, she speaks to John about whether or not to send Cristina to the school that Bernice attends. Listening carefully to Flor's concerns about the negative elements of this school for the rich, he admits to sharing her misgivings. She is of course surprised that he has not tried to convert her to his way of life, as Deb does continually. Reluctantly, he ends the conversation by complimenting her on her English, saying, 'It has been a pleasure to meet you.' Unaware, John has fallen in love with Flor by way of her female language – one is reminded of the moment earlier when after secretly letting out Bernice's new clothes she says to Bernice – in a phrase heavily rehearsed with Cristina – 'jes' try it on', a remark Bernie comes to love because it typifies Flor's distinctly female language. When Flor leaves the house for the last time, Bernie is in the swimming pool. Dripping wet and crying, she wants to embrace Flor but is afraid of splashing her clothes. Flor opens her arms, saying, 'Get me wet.'

The nature of the relationship between John and Flor only becomes clear after Deb has admitted to her affair, and John, desperate to get away from the house, takes Flor to his restaurant. Instead of making love to her, he cooks for her. After enjoying watching him work and savouring the inspired meal, she sees his sense of responsibility coming to the fore, the very element she so admires in him. And it is clear he sees precisely the same commitment on her part to her daughter. Instead of consummating their love, she confesses her love, and he admires her beauty, not just that of her outward appearance but of her inner being. Meanwhile, back at the house, mother-in-law (Cloris Leachman) has sobered up and warns her daughter that she is about to lose her husband. When Deb replies, 'Once again, Mother, you have lowered my self-esteem', her mother responds with one of the great examples of female language of the film: 'At moments like these your low self-esteem is simply a measure of your good common sense.' Later, when Deb is agonising about what is happening between Flor and John at the restaurant, her mother tells her – another great female line – that there are worse things than finding out that you love your husband. The next and final scene is when Flor takes Cristina away from the Claskys and tells her she will not go to Bernice's school.

What they leave behind is an American upper-middle-class world fraught with anxieties, symbolised by the constant jogging of the inhabitants, forever running aimlessly to and fro. After Cristina has demanded in anger as they leave the Claskys, 'to have my own space', a phrase typical of upper-middle-class American life, Flor instead offers a place in her heart that is constant, the still point of the turning wheel. And now, having reached college age, Cristina seems to have profited from that boundless love. She is well enough adjusted to be proud of her Mexican heritage, of her mother's past hardships, and to have done well enough in school to qualify for possible admission to Princeton. Like John Clasky, Flor provides her family with stability and a refusal to accept any accomplishment or distraction that takes them away from their family. At one point, John wishes for three and one half stars rather than four so he can get on with his family life and not be bothered by 'rock star' fame. And the film concludes by suggesting that John and Flor will keep their feet and those of their family firmly on the ground.

Kristeva suggests a problem for women in the second phase. The upper-middle-class world of the Claskys is where all the political advancements for women are to be found and enjoyed, beginning with a superior education that leads to meeting and possibly marrying the 'right' man and getting a good job or gaining entry to a prestigious profession. And Flor comes to understand the significance of finding one's place in this world because she learns English, enabling her to have a conversation with John. Without the language of the culture, Flor had hardly existed or only existed by way of her daughter's English. Yet now when Flor has come into her own she takes Cristina away from the world that contains the best opportunities for her daughter's future. The problem is summed up by the mother-in-law, who remarks to Flor as she is leaving, 'with my daughter [Deb], I lived for myself. You live for your daughter, but

neither way works.' The price of success in this culture is the temptation, even the necessity of leaving others, particularly your loved
ones and family members, behind or neglected. And the alternative,
pursued by Flor, is that you restrict your child's desire for success.
Nevertheless, Flor takes Cristina out of that environment not so
much for herself but so that her daughter will not end up alone
without any family. And so the application to Princeton represents
an alternative, a young woman who turned her back on privilege to
remain true to her mother.

What will happen if she receives a scholarship to Princeton?
Will her mother not feel alienated in such an environment or has
Cristina reached a stage of maturity that may enable her to avoid
excluding her mother? The film suggests that John and Deb will
resolve their problems out of family love, for one another and
for their children. More importantly, having clearly fallen in love
with one another, John and Flor refuse to consummate their relationship out of loyalty to their families. They share a tolerance
for difference; John does not want his daughter badgered about
her weight, and Flor alters her clothes so she does not need to go
on a diet. The implication – and it is only an implication – is that
the culture has to make way for difference, in John's words with
regard to Bernice and Cristina, 'between odd and fitting in you
have to go for odd', another example of John's manly version of
female language. Cristina's application essay to Princeton has not
only a female voice but also female language that derives in part
from her mother's Spanglish, the language familiar to her since
she was twelve years old. Now, however, she speaks with a perfect accent and flawless grammar, demonstrating that she grew
up learning how to combine her Mexican past with her American
present. Her application must stand out as very different from the
others, suggesting that Cristina is a student who will learn without losing a sense of herself, profit from her professors but also
teach them about herself and her Spanglish upbringing. Kristeva
suggests that this kind of education requires a female language.
We are left to wonder where does that leave Flor; will her daughter as a Princeton graduate still speak her language? This issue is
considered in the third phase or generation, Kristeva's term for the
reintegration of women into the male world as equals not only
physically but also mentally.

Phase three: creatures and creatresses in Stephen Frears' *Philomena* (2013) and Lasse Halström's *The Hundred-Foot Journey* (2014)

This third state for Kristeva is an ideal that she advocates and one that she believes can be realised in our lives.

> In this third attitude, which I strongly advocate – which I imagine? – the very dichotomy man/woman as an opposition between two rival entities may be understood as belonging to *metaphysics*. What can 'identity', even 'sexual identity', mean in a new theoretical and scientific space where the very notion of identity is challenged? I am not simply suggesting a very hypothetical bisexuality which, even if it existed, would only, in fact, be the aspiration toward the totality of one of the sexes and thus an effacing of difference. What I mean is, first of all, the demassification of the problematic of *difference*, which would imply in a first phase, an apparent de-dramatization of the 'fight to the death' between rival groups and thus between the sexes. And this not in the name of some reconciliation – feminism has at least had the merit of showing what is irreducible even deadly in the social contract – but in order that the struggle, the implacable difference, the violence be conceived in the very place where it operates with the maximum intransigence, in other words, in personal and sexual identity itself, so as to make it disintegrate in its very nucleus (Kristeva, 209).

Phase three and Philomena

Philomena begins with a man and woman, Martin Sixsmith (Steve Coogan) and Philomena Lee (Judi Dench), as far apart as sexual difference itself. He is an upper-middle-class Oxford-educated political insider, journalist and BBC newscaster. She is of a lower class with little education and even less understanding of his professional environment. Although both are Catholics, she has maintained her faith whereas he has lapsed in his belief, overtly opposing some central doctrines of the Church. Moreover, their personalities and sensibilities are radically different. Philomena is kind, gentle, forbearing, tolerant of and interested in others, only losing her temper when people are very unkind. Martin, by contrast, is wary, sceptical, even cynical, quick to lose his temper and dismissive of fools.

They come together because each experiences an injustice. Philomena is thwarted in her efforts to find her son, who had been put up for adoption after his birth at a Catholic institution for 'fallen women'. Martin has been dismissed from his position for, as he puts it, 'something [he] did not say' because it is expedient for the politicians in power to blame him for their mistakes. Clearly, both the secular and the religious public worlds where women in phases one and two have made their progress have failed Philomena and Martin. Not surprisingly, Philomena refuses to blame the 'sisters' as she calls them, but Martin's persistence leads her to find out about her son and to realise that the nuns have lied to her.

The process of finding out about Philomena's son involves the combination of male and female characteristics described above by Kristeva. At first indifferent to Philomena as a person, Martin becomes interested in selling her 'human interest' story, but Philomena is understandably reluctant to have her privacy invaded. After some give and take on both their parts, they begin to work as a team, a combination that proves successful in the visit to Pete Olson, her son Michael's former lover. Olson steadfastly refuses to speak to Martin; even when 'doorstepped', as Martin puts it, he will not let him in or answer any questions. Reluctantly, Philomena knocks on the door. Taken aback at the presence of a mother explaining that she simply wants to know about her son, Olson opens his door to them. It is important to keep in mind that prior to this meeting Philomena had given up, believing that Anthony/Michael – the former is his birth name and the latter is that given him by his adopted parents – never thought or cared about her or his Irish roots. Martin makes her persist, but his masculine aggression at the door puts Olson off. Less aggressive, quietly persistent, Philomena gets through the door, even though Martin got her to the door.

The interview with Olson is the turning point of the film, for here Philomena and Martin not only find out the details of Anthony/Michael's life as an adult in the United States but also discover that he journeyed back to Ireland in search of his mother and was in fact buried – his dying wish – at Roscrea, the place where he was born and spent time with his birth mother, Philomena. The story of the life of Anthony/Michael is now complete, and the question becomes what is to be done with it and about it. The final scene at Roscrea, when all is now clear to Philomena and Martin, reveals an important development in what Kristeva calls the sexual 'nucleus' of both. Martin forces his way into Sister Hildegarde's apartment to confront her with his question: Why did you lie to this poor man seeking his mother before dying of AIDS? Sister Hildegarde defends herself by saying that these women, unlike her, did not preserve their chastity and deserved the punishment they received. Martin replies that Christ, if he were present, would have tipped her out of her wheelchair. Philomena does not agree: she pardons Sister Hildegarde, explaining that she does not want to hate people. Martin replies that he is angry, to which Philomena responds, 'That must be exhausting.' It would seem they are at loggerheads, particularly as Martin's parting line to Sister Hildegarde is, 'I do not forgive you.'

The film does not end there. Calming down, Martin buys an effigy of Jesus, finds Philomena at the gravestone of her son and gives her the statue, a sign of respect for her faith. Thanking him, she places it on the gravestone. Martin then informs Philomena that he has decided not to publish the story because it is, in his view, a private matter. Then Philomena surprises him, explaining that she wants other people to know her story. Not wishing to bear a grudge against Sister Hildegarde, she also does not want what happened to her to recur. The journalistic element of Martin has had its effect upon her, as Philomena's refusal to dwell in anger has had upon him. In short, Martin has taken on board a feminine element, an unwillingness to harbour anger. And Philomena has taken on a masculine characteristic, an unwillingness to let the nuns bury the past. The nucleus of their beings has been sundered. And so the film itself combines their beings. We have, on the one hand, a sympathetic portrait of a woman who is deprived of her child by the Church that she continues to honour, a faith that underlies a personality of loving kindness, decency, and honesty. On the other hand, we have Martin, a shrewd journalist, insistent on finding the truth but not without principles and not without, as we see in the end, heart. That combination is what solves the mystery of the life of Anthony/Michael.

As Kristeva had predicted, the personalities of Martin and Philomena remain as distinct and as sexually different as ever. After they leave Roscrea for the last time, Philomena tells Martin the story of a romantic novel with a plot reminiscent of that of another such novel she had told him about earlier. On the previous occasion when she offered to lend him the book, he retorted, 'I feel as though I have read it already', a joke lost on Philomena but not on us. Now when the same offer is repeated, we come to understand that Philomena's devotion to these romances helps her maintain her cheerful and kind disposition in spite of the great injustice done to her. Martin is unlikely to be converted to this kind of fiction; he maintains his interest in what must in every way be in contrast to it, Russian history. Indeed, the interest in history as opposed to romance helps us understand how Martin Sixsmith's book differs from the film.

Unlike the movie, the book focuses less on Philomena and more on Anthony/Michael as a gay man in the Republican world of the Bush Sr. and Reagan administrations, reflecting his own victimisation in the world of power politics. In fact, the book version historicises the problem of combining male and female by placing the problem in the late twentieth-century United States when the federal government withheld medication for AIDS, something only mentioned in passing in the film. So Michael, like his mother, was being punished for his sexual activities, attitudes that now seem dated, of a past generation. This third generation, Kristeva hopes, is ready to move beyond that position. And Michael's serving loyally in the Bush and Reagan administrations is analogous to his mother's continued belief and trust in the Church. Avoiding male aggression and female passivity, Anthony/Michael leaves the United States in search of his birth mother with the intention of being buried at Roscrea, the place of his birth, not wishing to blame the Church or his mother. I suspect that most viewers feel, as I do, less forgiving of the sisters of Roscrea than does Philomena.

The film leaves us in some doubt as to whether Philomena's religious life or Martin's secular approach is to be preferred. We are left with sheer difference. Kristeva has a stronger position on the matter:

> The elements of the current practice of feminism that we have just brought to light (phase three) seem precisely to constitute such a representation which makes up for the frustrations imposed upon women by the anterior code (Christianity or its lay humanist variant). The fact that this new ideology has affinities, often revindicated by its creators, with so-called matriarchal beliefs … should not overshadow

its radical novelty. This ideology seems to me to be part of the broader anti-sacrificial current which is animating our culture (Kristeva, 208).

Kristeva believes that the present generation of feminist mothers has turned away from religion 'whose discourse tried and proved over thousands of years, provided the necessary ingredients for satisfying the anguish, the suffering, and the hopes of mothers' for a secular 'difficult and delightful apprenticeship in attentiveness, gentleness' (206). This new secular kind of mothering is seen in our next film, *The Hundred-Foot Journey*.

Phase three and The Hundred-Foot Journey

The Hundred-Foot Journey begins with a competitive relation-ship between the two restaurant owners, Madame Mallory (Helen Mirren) and Papa Kadam (Om Puri) and between the two would-be chefs, Marguerite (Charlotte Le Bon) and Hassan (Manish Dayal). Although the restaurant owners at first show overt aggression towards one another while the chefs display friendly competition, we should keep in mind William Blake's insight that love and hate are near allied. And that the true opposite of love is indifference. The point of the title is that the distance between love and hate, aggression and cooperation is very small but no less difficult to cross. Hassan is the key figure here; he is not only a talented student chef but also the only one of the main characters who never resorts to anger. In that sense he is a surrogate for his mother (Farzana Dua Elahe), who taught him to cook and who loved and was loved by all in the family. Hassan's talent as a chef combines male and female; he brings his mother's Indian taste together with his own desire to learn French cuisine. And he eventually stands out as one of the great innovators of French fine cuisine because of his unique combination of East and West, symbolised by the final meal that is cooked in Madame Mallory's kitchen but served in Papa Kadam's restaurant.

Hassan's ability to love the other while maintaining his own iden-tity, his intermingling male and female, is also the catalyst for the relationship between Madame Mallory and Papa Kadam. The turn-ing point is the restaurant fire, the culmination of acts of vandalism against Papa's restaurant that include slurs daubed on the walls of the restaurant. Horrified by this behaviour, Madame Mallory herself attempts to wash off the wall, dismisses the chef implicated in setting the fire, and offers to train Hassan in the 'classics' of French cuisine. When Papa objects that the Indian and French ways of cooking can never be combined, she replies that is precisely the sort of biased view that she has been struggling to erase from the wall in front of his restaurant. Hassan surprises her by using the Indian spices his mother left for him and using them not as the French recommend, in delicate 'pinches', but in generous Indian proportions. And she marvels at the brilliance of the tastes he produces. Once he has convinced his father to let him go to Madame Mallory's for six months of training, Hassan becomes the bonding agent between the two rival restaurateurs, and the friendship blossoms into a love affair that has at once a French and an Indian element. In a moment of relaxation, Papa refers to Madame Mallory as his 'almost girlfriend'. Suddenly, Madame without speaking leaves the table, rushing across the road to her restaurant. Fearing that she may be offended, Papa hurries over to apologise, only to find her waiting, arms outstretched, inviting him to dance with, as she quips, his 'almost girlfriend'. A bit of French savoir-faire joins with Indian forthrightness.

Finally, after Hassan has enjoyed his time in Paris at the top of the culinary world, reminded by one of his fellow workers from India of his origins, he decides to return to the French village of his family, that is, of his father and his adopted French mother. He wants to form a partnership with Marguerite. Together, they will manage Madame Mallory's restaurant and earn their third star. Although Hassan's distinctive cuisine combines two females, his Indian mother and his adopted French mother, he is quite ambitious and quietly sure of himself in a way usually considered typically male. At the same time, he adopts what is often seen as a typically female characteristic; avoiding confrontation, he always tries to find a peaceful means of resolving differences. When, after Papa opens his rival restaurant, Marguerite announces that they are at war, he smiles and responds disarmingly, 'Let battle begin.' Eventually Marguerite loans him her French cookbooks and gives him tips about how to cook the local produce; even she cannot find it in herself to battle with Hassan, who, as she admits after tasting his sauces, is more of a chef than anyone she has ever known. At the heart of Hassan's art of avoiding conflict is his deep self-esteem; his gift or talent is that he is at peace with his surroundings, the animal and vegetable worlds that make up the ingredients of his dishes, including his own love and that of those who love him.

Nevertheless, although it is abundantly clear that Marguerite and Hassan are deeply in love with one another, instead of proposing marriage he offers her an equal partnership in the restaurant, indicating his respect for her professional abilities. Kristeva reminds us that Freud pointed out that true love does not want to possess the other but to set her or him free. Cooking in the sense of fine cuisine in this film is seen to combine the male and female in the single nucleic self of a chef; combining the predominantly male drive for innovation with the female insistence on the maintenance of refined, classic taste. Hassan as a chef becomes the son of Mama and Madame Mallory.

Recently, when I lectured on this film to a group of postgraduate students studying in Paris, they characterised the film as, in their terms, a bit 'cheesy'. Eventually, I came to understand that this term meant that the rapprochement that developed between the two families was unrealistic, unlikely to happen in present-day France. And I accept their judgement, since they were long-time residents of a country where I was merely a fortunate if fleeting visitor. Kristeva speaks to this point, namely that literature, by which I believe she means the arts in general, opens up our world to possibilities that we cynical realists regard as unlikely, bringing us to see that they are not as improbable as we had thought. Kristeva suggests that for this reason women's desire for affirmation manifests itself in what she calls literature.

> Is it because, faced with social norms, literature reveals a certain knowledge and sometimes the truth itself about an otherwise repressed, nocturnal, secret and unconscious universe? ... This identification with the potency of the imaginary ... bears witness to woman's desire to lift the weight of what is sacrificial in the social contract from their shoulders ... to name the enigmas of the body, the dreams, secret joys, shames, hatreds of the second sex (Kristeva, 207).

By extension, art opens up our world to possibilities deemed improbable and relegated to the unconscious or to fantasy but in so doing taps into a resource for change. For Kristeva, the possibility of the third phase of feminism, combining male and female, ending feminism as such, resides in the cultural unconscious. And a 'feel-good' film like *The Hundred-Foot Journey* plays upon that resource, that 'potency of the imaginary', whether or not it is ever realised. The film leaves me, however, with a more specific imaginary scene than that of a split sexual nucleus. The partnership of Hassan and Marguerite will undoubtedly lead to a third Michelin star and, I would like to think, a large and happy family like the Kadam family at a dining table like that of Marguerite, who will be a fine chef/mother. This table reminds me of the early scene in the film when Marguerite rescues the Kadams, stranded on the roadside, tows their van into town, and treats them to fresh fruits and vegetables from her larder. That initial gesture of hospitality and good will shows Marguerite to be both a potential chef and mother; the foodstuffs on the table are the best from the local area, fresh and unspoiled by unnecessary garnish. Her open smile and generosity make the family feel at ease almost as if in the presence of their own mother.

Marguerite's career has been different from that of Hassan. She remains at home while he goes off to Paris to achieve national fame and fortune. Hassan could not have done it without the three women in his life: his mother who nourished his cooking talent; Madame Mallory, who provided his culinary training; and Marguerite, who gave him his first French cookbooks and told him, 'You are more of a chef than anyone I have ever met.' Hassan never forgets these women; early in the movie, he explains to the immigration official that he does have proper qualifications as a cook, having learned from his mother. And he leaves Paris to return to Madame Mallory's restaurant to strive for a third star, inviting Marguerite to be his partner in this endeavour. But Marguerite has not achieved fame: as she points out to him after the second star is awarded, 'They want you, not us.' And here we confront the cultural dilemma of women in our society. Had she, not Hassan, been the head chef recruited to go to Paris, would she have had the opportunity to marry and have a family? And is the career–mother combination a satisfactory alternative to father–fame? The question remains unresolved but demonstrates that breaking down the sexual nucleus does not eliminate sexual difference. In the next chapter, Homi K. Bhabha considers subservience in a larger sense, including that of all oppressed groups.

4 Homi K. Bhabha: post-colonial hybridity

Like Kristeva, Bhabha takes interpretation for granted but insists that the point of view of the oppressed/oppressor must be included in the interpretive perspective. Hybridity is his term for this state of mind, which for him assumes three forms: (1) hybridity as identity as portrayed in The Butler *and* Belle; *(2) hybridity as power as seen in* 12 Years a Slave *and* Django Unchained; *(3) hybridity as blasphemy exemplified in* Breaking Bad *and* Sherlock.

Born in 1949 in Bombay, Homi K. Bhabha, Anne F. Rothenberg Professor of English and American Literature at Harvard University, was raised and received his BA in post-colonial India, in the shade of the fire temple. He then went to Oxford University for his advanced degrees. His theory focuses upon the relationship between the colonised and the coloniser, which for Bhabha are always intertwined, never separate, and therefore related to the general situation of minority versus majority, submissive versus dominant in all cultures.

In his major work, *The Location of Culture* (1994), Bhabha develops most fully his concept of hybridity, the subject of this chapter. He began to formulate and use the notion of hybridity in the previous decade. Originally a botanical term, hybridity focuses on the intertwining of the perspectives of colonised and coloniser, indicating that the master and slave relationship, however it grows and evolves, remains in one sense unchanged. Even after colonialism and slavery have ended, the scar of hybridity never wholly disappears from the psyche of overseer and underling in part because it is a part of the history of the culture, as are segregation and slavery in the United States, apartheid in South Africa, colonialism in

Europe. Moreover, the constancy of hybridity is related to the fact that these hierarchical relationships were always ambivalent:

> The colonial presence is always ambivalent, split between its appearance as original and authoritative and its articulation as repetition and difference ... Such a display of difference produces a mode of authority that is agonistic (rather than antagonistic) and produces the split subjects of the racist stereotype (such as) the simian Negro or the effeminate Asiatic male (Bhabha, 153).

The dialectical concept of self/other and the phenomenological projection of otherness are unstable states, phases of philosophical development that in principle lead beyond themselves. Hybridity, on the other hand, according to Bhabha, is a relatively stable state in that the individual cannot advance beyond it because, in addition to the personal scar, the 'ambivalence' is embedded in their culture. For this reason, Bhabha's concept is illustrated by and deeply bound up with literary presentations of various cultures where the evolution that dialecticians and phenomenologists would expect has not occurred. For literary criticism, Bhabha's notion has particular utility in the analysis of literary characters, especially in their relation to the social hierarchy of their culture. In a more general sense beyond the literary, hybridity applies to anyone's response to authority. This chapter will consider three elements of Bhabha's concept of hybridity: hybridity as identity, hybridity as power, and hybridity as blasphemy.

Hybridity as identity: Lee Daniel's *The Butler* (2013) and Amma Asante's *Belle* (2013)

I begin with identity because Bhabha locates personal identity at the meeting point between literature and the post-colonial experience, that is, between literature or literary theory and life, a crossroads that Bhabha calls 'worldling'.

> The study of world literature might be the study of the way in which cultures recognise themselves through their projections of 'otherness'. ... The centre of such a study would neither be the 'sovereignty' of national cultures, nor the universalism of human culture, but a focus

on those 'freak and social displacements' ... which lead us to ask: can
the perplexity of the unhomely, interpersonal world lead to an international theme (Bhabha, 17).

For Bhabha, personal alienation of the colonised or displaced
individual – particularly as portrayed in art – may provide a
means towards understanding the relations between cultures
since he believes that the colonial situation always involves an
intermingling of the private and public, of the psychological and
the sociological.

> If we are seeking a 'worlding' of literature, then perhaps it lies in a crit-
> ical act that attempts to grasp the sleight of hand with which literature
> conjures with historical specificity, using the medium of psychic uncer-
> tainty, aesthetic distancing, or the obscure signs of the spirit world, the
> sublime and subliminal. As literary creatures and political animals, we
> ought to concern ourselves with the understanding of human action
> and the social world as a movement when *something is beyond con-
> trol but not beyond accommodation* ... the critic must attempt to fully
> realise, and take responsibility for, the unspoken, unrepresented pasts
> that haunt the historical present (Bhabha, 17–18).

Art for Bhabha has access, or more accurately provides us with
access, to the unwritten, the unspoken, since so much of the
oppression suffered by the subordinate is not recorded, not considered of historical import at the time of its occurrence, if ever.
In the shadow of art, between the lines so to speak, lurks a lurid,
repressed past that is made apparent for Bhabha in the artistic
relations shown between past and present, the individual and the
social.

> Private and public, past and present, the psyche and the social develop
> an interstitial intimacy. It is an intimacy that questions binary divi-
> sions through which such spheres of social experience are often spa-
> tially opposed. These spheres of life are linked through an 'in-between'
> temporality that takes the measure of dwelling at home, while pro-
> ducing an image of the world as history ... And the inscription of this
> borderline existence inhabits a stillness of time and a strangeness of
> framing that creates the discursive 'image' at the crossroads of history
> and literature, bridging the home and the world (Bhabha, 19).

Bhabha describes this artistic phenomenon by way of a literary portrait of a black woman living during Apartheid.

> Through this painterly distance a vivid strangeness emerges, a partial
> or double 'self' is framed in a climactic political moment that is also
> a contingent historical event ... They had to recognise her but *what*
> do they recognise in her? Words will not speak and the silence freezes
> into the image of apartheid: identity cards, police frame-ups, prison
> mug-shots, the grainy press pictures of terrorists (Bhabha, 20).

Bhabha explains that the 'stillness' of this literary portrait, 'its obscure necessity', helps us grasp what 'Emanuel Levinas has magically described as the twilight existence of the aesthetic image – art's image as 'the very event of obscuring a descent into night, an invasion of the shadow' (Bhabha, 21–2). The 'completion' of the aesthetic, the distancing of the world in the image, is precisely not a transcendental activity. The image or the metaphoric 'fictional' activity of discourse makes visible an 'interruption of time by a movement going on on the hither side of time, in its interstices' (21–2).

Bhabha employs Levinas to explain how art is especially adept at locating these intersections between the individual and the 'unhomely' culture, that is, the place that is supposed to be home but evokes discomfort. Bhabha is drawn to Levinas' notion that art frames history, often subtly and inconspicuously, within an ethical context where the home or context of the story or picture is seen as unhomely.

> The aesthetic image discloses an ethical time of narration because,
> Levinas writes, 'the real world appears in the image as it were between
> parentheses' ... (which) effects an 'externality of the inward' as the
> very enunciative position of the historical and narrative subject ...
> it is this ethical-aesthetic positioning that returns us, finally, to the
> community of the unhomely (Bhabha, 22).

Hybridity as identity in The Butler

I turn now to two films to illustrate these complex ideas. A scene near the conclusion of *The Butler* illustrates the above notion of the ethical-aesthetic positioning of the unhomely. In one of the last scenes of the film, Cecil (Forest Whitaker) and his wife Gloria (Oprah Winfrey), now well into retirement, visit the plantation of his youth. An eerie stillness pervades the scene that was once a hive of exploited industry. Cecil remarks, 'We Americans ignore our own wrongs, condemning Nazi concentration camps while permitting similar sites of racist suffering two centuries before Hitler came to power.' An autobiographical moment, one of personal history for Cecil, is framed by an ethical-aesthetic image of injustice, of the unhomely, the key element of which is seen at the beginning of the film during the butler's childhood experience in the cotton field when the white master rapes his mother and murders his father. Before we turn to that scene, it is important to keep in mind that the ethical-aesthetic framing device is set up at the beginning and end of the film. Before any pictures appear on the screen, we see the words of Martin Luther King: 'Darkness cannot drive out darkness. Only light can do that', and at the end of the film after all the images fade away, words again appear on the screen: 'This film is dedicated to those men and women who fought for our freedom in the Civil Rights Movement.' The butler's home is rendered unhomely by slavery in the South and racism in the North. Cecil's story is thus to be seen as a miniature form of the Civil Rights Movement: this ethical-aesthetic positioning of the butler's life places the unhomely world of Cecil in history. In the end, when Cecil walks along the corridor of the White House to meet President Obama, explaining to the black official at his side, 'I know the way', we are left to ponder the fact that Cecil was there before Obama and may have helped in a small way to pave the way for the first black president of the United States of America.

Throughout most of the film, Cecil did not wish in any way to be associated with the Civil Rights Movement or any other political group favouring radical change in US race relations. The reason for his attitude is made clear in the opening scene when Cecil is suddenly orphaned: his father is murdered, and his violated mother never speaks again. The audience is here introduced to hybridity. From the perspective of the stunned young man, we dwell for a moment within his world, looking without, experiencing his unhomely home, too real to be unreal. From our other perspective without we are outraged at this cruel, criminal act but recognise that the boy is wholly powerless. Indeed, when the master's wife offers to take him into the house and train him as a

'house nigger' he has no choice but to accept. Ironically, this act
of what might be called eccentric even perverse kindliness leads
to his freedom and to his becoming a butler. Despite this fact, the
slave home remains decidedly unhomely. As his father says to him
a few moments before dying, 'This is the white man's world; we
just live in it.' And that is precisely the position of the black butler.
Cecil's hybridity derives from seeing and hearing but behaving as
if he were deaf and dumb, for that is what he is trained to do from
the moment he becomes a house slave, an instruction reiterated
by his superiors at the White House.

This dual or hybrid perspective is crucial to understanding the
dilemma of a slave. Indeed, Cecil's father prevents his young son
from trying to protect his mother and then himself stands up to the
master only to be unceremoniously killed, making only too clear
why he prevented his son from reacting. This dreadful scene can
only be comprehended by way of what Bhabha names 'the external-
ity of the inward': from within, the father knows that the external
response to the son trying to save his mother would undoubtedly
be futile, resulting possibly in the loss of the son's life. Yet the father
cannot prevent himself from defending his wife, a response that
is probably both instinctive and founded on the external cultural
belief – evoked when his son asks his daddy, 'What you gonna
do?' – that the husband must defend his wife.

This duality haunts Cecil throughout his life. And Bhabha is at
pains to stress that this type of duality can never be transcended;
nor is it part of a dialectic to be overcome. No. The hybrid is always
a hybrid. In fact, the position of butler is itself marked by such a
duality, a servant and subservient yet required to maintain the external appearance of personal dignity and self-respect. The film places
Cecil in an 'ethical-aesthetic' position particularly with regard to
his family. Although paid a salary well below that of his Caucasian
equivalent, Cecil manages to provide a decent home for his family
and educate his two boys. The price of his hard work is that he is
seldom home: his wife becomes an alcoholic, his elder son grows
alienated from the white establishment world, and his younger son
escapes from the unhomely home by volunteering for military service in Vietnam. In short, we see the disintegration of his family, particularly when his wife has an affair with the neighbour, the elder
son becomes a Black Panther, and the younger boy is killed in battle.
The ethical dilemma aesthetically framed here is that in serving his

president the butler neglects his family, the members of which each suffer in different ways.

The hybrid duality is most vivid in the relationship between Cecil and his eldest son, Louis. While the father politely asks his superior for pay equal to that of a white man and is told to look elsewhere for employment if he is dissatisfied with his salary, the son participates in a sit-in against segregation. Cecil believes that Louis's aggression against the establishment is futile and dangerous. Louis sees his father as an 'Uncle Tom', remaining subservient even when his plea for equal pay for black employees at the White House is for years ignored. Father and son each have an element of the other in themselves, making it possible eventually for them to comprehend themselves in the other, what Wittgenstein called 'family resemblance'. The differences between them are extreme until the end of the film. The main distinction derives from the fact that Cecil was born a slave, having to make his way without any family. Louis, by contrast, grows up in a loving family with sufficient education to realise that he is entitled to the same opportunities as white men. Cecil feels that militant opposition to white abuse will only produce more violence, and Louis believes that placating the white man will result in the status quo being maintained. The basis for their disagreement is an understanding of the other. Bhabha's notion of the relationship between the public and private, between the 'dwelling at home' and the 'image of the world as history' is particularly apt here. For the film takes us through the progress of race relations in the United States from the administration of Eisenhower to that of Obama. And the change in the historical situation affects and is affected by the personal. Cecil gradually becomes more overt in his opposition to the establishment until he finally resigns from his position at the White House, while Louis grows less militant, turning away from violent confrontation to peaceful political protest. In the end when father and son finally embrace they are able tacitly to recognise that each contains an element of the other.

Both struggle with different forms of hybridity. Louis insists that the world must change more rapidly than his parents believe possible but discovers that he is unwilling to kill to achieve that end and so turns from the Black Panthers to politics. Cecil attempts to achieve justice for black people at the White House by appealing to the decency of his boss, but his words fall on deaf ears until he appeals to President Reagan, who forces Cecil's immediate superior to do what he otherwise would not. This Pyrrhic victory combined with the disintegration of his family leads Cecil to reconsider. When he decides to retire, President Reagan, in a moving and personal moment, expresses doubt about his own opposition to the Civil Rights Movement. Stepping out of his role as a butler for the first time, Cecil replies, 'I used to be scared. I'm trying now not to be so scared any more.' In the next scene we see Cecil, after his resignation from the White House, joining his son in front of the South African Embassy in a protest against Apartheid.

The reconciliation of father and son does not represent the end of hybridity. Rather, it involves a sharing of the same kind of hybridity. Louis now protests but in a political and non-violent way, a strategy he learned from Martin Luther King. And we should remember what King said about men like Louis's father, that black domestic servants gave a dignity and trustworthiness to the image of the black man that contributed positively to the struggle for equality. Cecil, for his part, has moved beyond being a butler. When he visits Obama wearing the tie given to him by Mrs Kennedy and his tiepin from Lyndon Baines Johnson (LBJ), he marches now as an old soldier of the Civil Rights war, limping and scarred but dignified and, in a sense, decorated with his domestic medals. Like all warriors, he lives with the price of war. With his son he shares the hybridity that balances their losses of their son/brother, Charlie, and their wife/mother, Gloria, not to mention the clashes of their own past relationship, with the prospect of further struggle for Louis's children/Cecil's grandchildren to be faced by them with more mutual understanding and perhaps a little less fear.

The Butler leaves us with a question that moves beyond Bhabha. The first image we see of Cecil is during the opening credits. Dressed in a suit with his Kennedy tie and LBJ tiepin, he waits to meet President Obama. In the final scene, we see the continuation of this scene, Cecil walking towards the Oval Office to meet the first black president of the United States. As he walks firmly on weary limbs, a domestic war veteran, to meet Obama, we seem to be entering a new era of history, one in which a black butler is a war hero and the president of the most powerful country in the world is a black man. Hybridity remains but history changes. *The Butler* suggests that although hybridity remains its context may change radically with history.

Hybridity as identity in Belle

Belle is about female hybridity. Literally a hybrid, the child of a black slave mother and a white father, Belle (Gugu Mbatha-Raw) is constantly confronted by the duality of her position. At Kenwood House she is treated as the equal companion of her white cousin, Elizabeth (Sarah Gadon), but is not allowed to be at table with her on public occasions. Both young women are courted by brothers of the same aristocratic family, but Belle, unlike Elizabeth, is not allowed to 'come out', that is, appear in society as a young woman eligible for marriage. Belle struggles against these arbitrary restrictions, and her agon, not to say antagonism – to use Bhabha's terms – is again seen in ethical-aesthetic and historical terms. The problem is exacerbated by the fact that Lord Mansfield (Tom Wilkinson), the head of the household and Lord Chief Justice of Great Britain, offers each of the young women an equal share of his fatherly love, a fact which becomes apparent when the portrait that he has commissioned of the two is revealed to show them as equals and as equally beautiful in different ways. The painting is not only an aesthetic object of beauty and an ethical act of equality, it is also an historical artefact: until 1922 it actually hung in Kenwood House and is now at Scone Castle in Scotland. As an historical document the portrait indicates that, in the latter half of the eighteenth century, slavery was beginning to be called into question and that Lord Mansfield's decision on the *Zong* massacre, a ruling outlawing slaves being treated as mere cargo, is a landmark decision.

Belle's personal journey is also a struggle with ethical-aesthetic and historical aspects of hybridity. At first she accepts the proposal of marriage from Oliver Ashcroft (James Norton), believing that no one else would have her. When John Davinier (Sam Reid), the person whom she prefers, confesses his love for her, she breaks off her relationship with Ashcroft, agreeing to marry Davinier. However, Lord Mansfield and Davinier have had a falling out over the question of the justification of slavery. Eventually, Lord Mansfield's decision against slaves as cargo comes very close to Davinier's view that slavery itself is wrong, particularly when Mansfield, after announcing his legal decision, adds that slavery is so 'odious' as to be wholly without justification. Moreover, Mansfield decides to take Davinier into his chambers so that Belle will be marrying a gentleman.

The conclusion of *Belle*, however, is different from that of *The Butler*. Although slavery is being questioned, hybridity remains alive and well. The respectability of both Belle and Davinier resides in their being accepted as a couple by the Lord Chief Justice. But will people like the Ashcrofts also tolerate them? We are left in some doubt, particularly as the elder Ashcroft (Tom Felton) insulted and brutally fondled Belle even though he thought at that stage she was to be the wife of his brother. Hybridity in Great Britain takes a very different form from that in the United States of America. Cecil and his children and grandchildren must continue to struggle for civil rights because of the remnants not only of slavery but also more recently of segregation and well-nigh institutionalised racism represented by, for example, the Ku Klux Klan. The problem facing Belle and Davinier is subtler and more insidious. Although the legal rights of the black people were well established by Mansfield's decision, followed in 1834 by the outlawing of slavery in Great Britain, the problem of acceptance into society continued. The Ashcrofts, representative of the British establishment, with the exception of the youngest son who falls in love with Belle, have nothing but contempt for Belle and only find her marginally acceptable because of her inheritance and their desperate need of money. And it is important to recall that even after slavery was outlawed in Britain the profits of slavery else-where, particularly in the colonies, continued to be enjoyed by the British for over a century. This double standard would result in a personal hybridity for Belle and Davinier and their progeny, the sort of hybridity experienced by black immigrants to Britain for the past two centuries.

Perhaps the most interesting form of personal hybridity in *Belle* is that of Mansfield himself. Torn between the norms of social decorum and his deep love for Belle, and subject to the huge financial pressures of truly national proportions to protect the slave trade for British merchants, Mansfield makes a momentous decision. Although, as he maintains to Davinier, the *Zong* judgment is not the same as outlawing slavery, it is clearly a major step in that direction. And the result for Mansfield is that he has stood his ground against the head of the Ashcroft family (Alex Jennings), a prominent member of the political establishment. Yet even for Mansfield the social dilemma cannot be avoided; he feels unable to allow Belle to sit at table during public occasions and cannot permit her to marry someone who is not a gentleman.

Belle moves beyond Bhabha in suggesting how innovation occurs in a system based upon racism and slavery. Here the conversation between Mansfield and his wife is very important. While he rails against the presumptuousness and brashness of Davinier, Mrs Mansfield (Emily Watson) reminds him that he had similar ideas when he first entered the profession. She also reminds him that he once thought, as Davinier does, that he could change the world. In the end, he does just that, striking at the heart of slavery by asserting that people of any colour cannot be treated as 'cargo'. We cannot know, nor probably did Mansfield himself, if this decision was influenced by his love for Belle, though it is hard to believe that she did not have some effect upon his decision. We sense that as his own hybridity grows upon him, watching Belle develop into an elegant, intelligent young woman, he comes to have empathy with her form of hybridity. In contrast to the Mansfields, the Ashcrofts remain 'pure bred', aloof from and indifferent to Belle and her forebears. Paradoxically, hybridity seems here related to both the status quo and radical social change.

The love that develops between Belle and Mansfield is similar to that between Belle and her cousin Elizabeth. Ironically, Belle is rendered independently wealthy by her father's inheritance, but Elizabeth's father, who has remarried, leaves all to his new wife and nothing to his daughter. Elizabeth must find a husband who can afford to keep her. James Ashcroft becomes engaged to her when he believes that she is to come into the Mansfield inheritance. When he is disabused of this notion, he marries another woman without saying a word to Elizabeth. Belle is so upset at how her cousin has been treated that she decides to give half her inheritance to Elizabeth so that she will no longer be at the mercy of unscrupulous suitors. The wonderful irony here is that the mixed-race woman provides freedom to the white woman. To do justice to Elizabeth, she has always treated Belle as her equal and loved her as a sister. White and black hybridity hold something in common that may result in love across race lines. Hybridity in *Belle* is not merely a static part of one's identity but serves to foster both social and personal change. And, as we saw in *The Butler*, hybridity evolves, must evolve with the changing historical situation and hybridity contributes to historical change.

Hybridity as power: Steve McQueen's *12 Years a Slave* (2013) and Quentin Tarantino's *Django Unchained* (2012)

Since slavery is the most extreme form of subordination, Bhabha applies hybridity to slavery, assuming that the concept will also apply to lesser kinds of subordination. His point of departure is that slavery cannot be relegated to the past. We must not see racism 'as a hangover from archaic conceptions of the aristocracy, but as part of the historical traditions of civic and liberal humanism that create ideological matrices of national aspiration together with their concept of a ['people'] and its imagined community (Bhabha, 359).

Here it is well to remember that at the end of *12 Years a Slave* we are informed that even after Northrup is freed from his illegal servitude, his attempt to prosecute the two men who flouted the law, kidnapping and selling him into slavery, was unsuccessful. In spite of the laws against slavery, the society remains racist. Even now, I suspect, Bhabha would argue that the fact that slave films like *12 Years a Slave* and *Django Unchained* are box-office successes during the administration of the first black president of the United States demonstrates not that racism is behind us but that it remains deeply embedded in Western culture.

Hybridity as power in 12 Years a Slave
Solomon Northrup (Chiwetel Ejiofor) is so easily kidnapped and sold as a slave because he is trusting, naive, even a bit gullible, that is, wholly without any element of hybridity. Following the opening scene, to be discussed shortly, we are introduced to mid-nineteenth-century Saratoga, New York, where Northrup, a well-dressed family man, is clearly a respected member of the community. Living in the slave-free Northern state of New York, Northrup does not even consider the possibility of being a slave, and that is of course why he is such easy prey for the kidnappers. A successful violinist well respected in the community, Solomon is accustomed to taking the world as it presents itself. When the two performers compliment him on his reputation as a violinist and offer him a lucrative engagement in Washington, he takes them at their word, accepting their generous business proposition. After arriving in Washington, they entertain him lavishly, get him thoroughly drunk, and then carry him home in a semi-conscious state. A decent, law-abiding man, he never suspects any foul play until the next morning when he

awakens to find himself imprisoned and in chains. And from this point on we follow Northrup in his and our education into the terrifying and gory life of a slave.

As a slave, Northrup develops hybridity because it is necessary to his survival. At first, he is straight and one-dimensional with the slavers, asserting that he is a free and educated man. The result with most of his masters is that they do not believe him and punish him more severely than the other slaves. Even with the best of his slavers, Master Ford, who believes him, the result is unsatisfactory. Ford feels constrained by the conventions of the slave South and cannot or will not sacrifice his financial investment in Northrup as a slave. In short, the good master, whether willingly or not, is a slave of the system. However, Ford does reward Northrup for devising a means of transporting logs by water; he presents him with a violin, an instrument that gives Northrup a special place in the society and even enables him to earn a bit of money. The hard lesson Northrup learns from Ford is not to mention that he is different from the other slaves: he recognises that his survival as a slave requires that he pretend to be illiterate. What might at first seem to be duplicity or simply lying is really hybridity, that is, the pretence of illiteracy is always treated with doubt and scepticism because in his demeanour and manner of speaking he appears to be anything but illiterate. In short, Northrup learns to present the face of hybridity, the slave seeming to accept his enslavement, and at the same time the free man in fetters who ceases to declare his freedom.

Once Ford sells Northrup to Epps we enter the lowest rung of slave hell where hybridity is not merely an acceptable face in a slave world but necessary for survival. Epps' perverse wife asks Northrup if he is educated. When he denies having any schooling, she replies it is just as well because you will thereby escape extra whipping. Yet she chooses him as her shopping boy. The subtlety of hybridity is manifest here. Northrup shows Mrs Epps that he can balance the perspective of both slave and master or mistress: he is schooled in how to adopt the proper (unschooled) posture for Mrs Epps. For that reason she is intrigued by him, possibly perversely amused to see how he will use his slight bit of freedom – and, she may suspect, his education – as an errand boy. And, in fact, he nearly oversteps himself on his first outing, departing from his prescribed path, probably thinking about trying to escape, only to come upon two slaves being hanged, probably for attempting to escape, a very close call.

The final stage is beyond that of merely covering up, or what might be called the 'white' lie. When Armsby, a white man who works with the slaves, befriends Northrup, he offers him the small amount of money earned as a fiddler to deliver a letter to his friends in the North. Armsby, however, betrays Northrup, exposing him to Epps. In this pivotal scene, Epps has his arms wrapped ominously around Northrup's neck. Looking into Epps' eyes, Northrup lies convincingly, 'Who would I write to and where would I get pen and paper? Armsby is lying to get back in with you so he can be the overseer of your slaves.' We have here a vivid example of the use and practice of hybridity: Northrup recognises that Epps is a slaver who thinks the worst of everybody, so he is likely to accept this tale about Armsby. Moreover, he realises that Armsby would have little compunction about sacrificing a slave to his own ambition. The success of Northrup's ploy is to think simultaneously as white and black, as slaver and slave.

Now that Northrup has understood the mentality of the depraved Epps he has earned his place at the bottom of hell, and his reward, so to speak, is that he is forced by Epps to whip Patsey (Lupita Nyong'o), the most fragile of the slaves, who in her abject misery had begged Northrup to take her life. Reluctantly, Northrup takes the whip from Epps, but he is unable to finish the job of a slaver, throwing down the whip, since the hybrid balances the slaver with the slave. Moreover, this scene depicts the true horror of slavery. Patsey is the best of the cotton pickers and an attractive sexual object for Epps. Yet, at the encouragement of his envious wife, Epps beats Patsey nearly to death. The point is that slavery at its worst is not merely economic exploitation of black people ('slave labour') but white people at war with their very selves, hating what they love of their own being. No wonder Epps thinks the worst of others and no wonder Northrup realises that his very survival depends on his understanding of that perversity and playing upon it with his Armsby story.

The perverse nature of slavery was introduced in the film in the opening scene, an introduction to the daily life of slavery. We see Northrup harvesting sugar cane while the plantation owner sits in his carriage fanning himself. As daylight descends, the slaves are fed a paltry meal and sleep on the ground huddled together. The woman next to Northrup rolls over onto him, and a form of sex ensues that might be described as that of tired animality. In fact, the scene is immediately juxtaposed with a memory of one of real love between Northrup and his wife to emphasise the debased sexuality of the slave scene. Slavery, we come to understand, drains man, both slave and slaver, of humanity, or nearly so. After the sex, Northrup looks woebegone and lost while the woman quietly sobs. Both return unrequited to their desperate search for love. It is in these terms that we comprehend Epps, who rapes Patsey and then whips her nearly into extinction, punishing her and himself for his attraction to her.

12 Years a Slave suggests that hybridity in a slave situation does not maintain a balance, and here McQueen goes beyond Bhabha. In the end slavery produces a choice between the ultimate perversity of Epps and the insistent inner decency of Northrup. The final irony of Northrup's journey into hell is that having finally completed his education, having internalised the slave/slaver hybrid, he is suddenly set free. Nevertheless, upon returning home to his family he maintains an inner vestige of his terrible ordeal. Entering his home dressed as a gentleman, facing his family respectfully waiting to greet him, he apologises for his appearance as if he were still a field slave who did not belong in the house. Here we see, as Bhabha predicted, the means by which subordination, be it as a slave or a colonised subaltern, remains in the 'free' or post-colonial world. The film, however, suggests that Northrup's hybridity may be only the temporary remnant of slavery, a sort of involuntary gesture, the acquired habit of one accustomed to being a subordinate. For Bhabha, by contrast, hybridity is a part of any slave or colonial culture, equally present in slaves and those who empathise with slaves, an idea we are to recognise as part of our culture. The film, however, leaves us with an additional question. Can Northrup ever recover from feeling like a house slave in his own home? Bhabha's hybridity of power is a function of the power of culture, but *12 Years a Slave* leads us to wonder whether a form of power hybridity may be so embedded in a psyche that it no longer responds to or evolves with cultural change. Alternatively, Northrup's entrapment within his slave role may be only temporary; in time, he may develop a kind of hybridity like that of his family.

Hybridity as power in Django Unchained

Django (Jamie Foxx) is also an apprentice to hybridity as power, but as a slave he is a particularly apt pupil. His tutor, Dr King Schultz (Christoph Waltz), is more benign than Northrup's masters.

A German, Schultz is not a slaver but a bounty-hunter who soon discovers that Django is a crack shot and naturally adept at bounty-hunting. The affinity between bounty-hunting and slavery is that both require hybridity; indeed, Schultz's mixture of formal and 'down home' English spoken with a thick German accent is a hybrid dialect. Moreover, the art of bounty-hunting involves appearing to be harmless and friendly until an opportunity arises to disarm or shoot the victim, since the reward usually stipulates 'dead or alive'.

Recognising Django's natural ability at bounty-hunting, Schultz offers him a partnership in return for helping to free Django's beloved Broomhilda, known as Hildi (Kerry Washington), who is now a slave at Candyland. In the first encounter with the master of Candyland, hybridity is used with great skill by both Schultz and Django to bring about a meeting with Mr Candy (Leonardo DiCaprio) and to arouse his interest in them. To inveigle their way into Candyland they invent a pretext other than that of freeing Hildi, since release from slavery would be unacceptable to Candy, a cruel master wholly committed to total servitude. Having discovered that Mr Candy is a devotee of black wrestling to the death (Mandingo fighting), Schultz presents himself as a slaver interested in buying one of Candy's Mandingo fighters accompanied by Django acting the part of his slave overseer and Mandingo adviser. One of the most vivid instances of hybridity as power occurs when one of Candy's Mandingo slaves attempting to escape is, on Candy's order, eaten alive by dogs. Horrified at the idea of setting the dogs on the poor man, Schultz tries to stop it, but Django, realising that such an act of mercy would give them away, interrupts Schultz, encouraging Candy to do what clearly he wants to do. No one can know a cruel slaver better than a slave or, in this instance, an ex-slave like Django. Continuing to play the part of black slaver, Django rides on horseback beside Candy's slaves shuffling in chains. Aware that a black slaver has never before been seen by any of these people, Django must convince them that he is what he purports to be. On the one hand, he stands up to Candy's white overseer as if he considered himself whiter than white and, on the other hand, he convinces the slaves that he is crueller than any white slaver could hope to be. In each role, he must continually balance the perspective of slave and slaver, of white and black, thus intriguing Candy who is fascinated by cruelty like his own. Django immediately recognises the perverse quality of a white slaver like Candy, a quality that is made clear to us and Schultz by the means used to execute the escaped slave.

Candy is mesmerised by Django, but his black house servant
Stephen is more sceptical. Who better to recognise the hybridity of
a slave than another slave, particularly a house slave whose daily
life as a butler places him among both black and white people?
Realising that Django and Hildi have 'something going on', Stephen
alerts Candy. A gun battle ensues in which Schultz and Candy are
killed and Django is captured and sold into slavery. Now Django
is obliged to use Schultz's form of hybridity to gain his freedom.
Convincing the Australian slavers of his qualifications as a bounty
hunter, he promises to lead them to the collection of a small fortune if they free him. Once the other slaves back up Django's claim
that he originally came to Candyland as a slaver not a slave, the
Australians make a deal with Django to go for the bounty. So his
past hybridity serves him well in establishing his new hybridity. Of
course, once released, Django shoots the slavers, then heads back
to Candyland to retrieve Hildi. There he confronts Stephen, his old
enemy who, we should keep in mind, became a house servant probably because of a gammy leg. Instead of executing Stephen, Django
kneecaps him, leaving him in Candyland as it burns down. Django
reserves the special punishment of being incinerated in Candyland
for the slave whom Candy placed above all of his other slaves, suggesting that Stephen's hybridity is his own undoing, trapping him
within the house where he was a slave-butler, a white black man.
As Django departs, Stephen, now unable to walk, promises Django
that he will be caught and punished and that Candyland will go on
for ever. On all counts, Stephen is wrong. Candyland is destroyed
by Django, who as a free man with the recently freed Hildi by his
side watches it go up in flames. In the final scene of the film, Django
and Hildi on horseback turn towards the burning Candyland while
the horse does a little dance reminiscent of those performed by the
well-known mounts of Gene Autry and Roy Rogers. This allusion
to Autry and Rogers takes us back to the days of Schultz's youth, if
he, like so many Europeans, was brought up on American cowboy
movies. This final gesture announces that Django is now adopting
the hybridity of black ex-slave/white cowboy since Gene Autry and
Roy Rogers regularly saved lovely women like Hildi, though of a
lighter colour. And Tarantino's final reference is to Roy Rogers and
Gene Autry, both of a generation of cowboys along with the Lone
Ranger and Hopalong Cassidy, to mention only a few, who were
dedicated to protecting the innocent and vulnerable. Placing Django

within this genre of the good cowboys of a previous generation, Tarantino suggests that his protagonist has now progressed from slave/ex-slave to ex-slave/freer of slaves, such as Hildi and the other female slaves he liberates from Candyland.

Slave culture in *12 Years a Slave* is regionalised: the free man in New York state is a slave in Georgia. Less regionalised, *Django Unchained* calls our attention to the particularly cruel element of slavery in the United States. After the dogs have killed the runaway slave, Candy remarks to Django that Schultz looks a bit shocked. Django explains that Schultz, a foreigner, is not familiar with American slavery, implying that slavery in the United States was marked by a sort of gratuitous cruelty not seen in other cultures, or at least those known to Schultz. In addition, Tarantino historicises slavery by placing the freed Django in a sort of future that links to the past, making him a black Gene Autry or Roy Rogers. The difference between Steve McQueen and Quentin Tarantino is that while Northrup remains with the slave/slaver hybrid, Django in the end moves to a new stage, freed ex-slave/white cowboy. Each protagonist carries his experience of slavery into the present and future culture, but Tarantino suggests that with ingenuity and humour the remnant of the past evolves and adapts to a different culture, a different audience, and a different historical moment. The final horse dance in *Django Unchained* is, in its comical way, more hopeful than *12 Years a Slave*, suggesting a new kind of role for Django.

Hybridity as blasphemy: Vince Gilligan's *Breaking Bad*, series 1, episode 1 (2008) and Paul McGuigan's *Sherlock*, series 2, episode 1 (2012)

Having demonstrated how hybridity applies to the subjugation of minority members, I turn in this section to hybridity among the dominant class, the establishment. Bhabha explains that blasphemy goes well beyond denigrating the Scriptures and the sacred documents and traditions of religion:

> To blaspheme is not simply to sully the ineffability of the sacred name … (it) goes beyond the severance of tradition and replaces its claim to a purity of origins with a poetics of relocation and reinscription … (it) is not merely a misrepresentation of the sacred by the secular; it is

a moment when the subject matter or content of a cultural tradition is being overwhelmed or alienated ... Into the asserted authenticity or continuity of tradition, 'secular' blasphemy releases a temporality that reveals the contingencies, even the incommensurabilities involved in the process of social transformation (Bhabha, 322–3).

Hybridity as blasphemy in Breaking Bad, series 1, episode 1

The television series *Breaking Bad* clearly involves a form of blasphemy leading to social transformation. Walter White (Bryan Cranston), a chemistry teacher, becomes a producer and pusher of methamphetamines, blaspheming the law in general and, in particular, his own discipline of chemistry. Moreover, blaspheming against the ethics of teaching, he joins forces with one of his students, Jesse Pinkman (Aaron Paul), better known as 'Cap'n Cook', a drug addict who brews and sells illegal drugs. Before deciding to move into the world of crime, White struggled to make ends meet, supplementing his meagre teaching salary with a job at a car-wash garage. Dedicated to his family, he spends evenings and weekends working overtime to keep his head above water, with one disabled son and another child on the way. Clearly Walter suffers from what might be called 'White on White' exploitation.

Episode 1 begins in the chemistry classroom. Frustrated by students who have no interest in the subject, which White explains movingly as being about life itself, and exploited by his boss at his second job, the car-wash garage, Walter collapses, is taken to hospital and is diagnosed with inoperable lung cancer. Although he tells no one about this death sentence, we soon see a change in his personality, a new tendency towards blasphemy, first when he quits his job at the car wash, swearing at and giving the finger to his boss, and then in the clothing store when he physically assaults a young man who is ridiculing his disabled son. His social transformation is completed only after he is taken by his brother-in-law, a DEO (drug enforcement officer), to a drug bust where seeing for the first time a criminal's amateur laboratory he suddenly becomes aware of the vast amounts of money made by these individuals. Having watched his student, Jesse Pinkman, escape from the scene of the crime, Walter decides that he can learn the ropes of the trade from him.

The 'incommensurability' Bhabha mentions is seen at his surprise birthday party when the brother-in-law jokingly says of Walter, 'He has a brain the size of Wisconsin, but we don't hold that against him.' Walter's family clearly regards him as an extremely intelligent, if somewhat unworldly, dedicated schoolteacher. What could be more incommensurate with that kind of personality than that of a drug producer and pusher?

The process by which Walter learns from Jesse while guiding him into a safer and more lucrative form of the drug-producing business provides a vivid example of hybridity as blasphemy. Walter brings his chemical expertise and concern for safety to Jesse, who has the street knowledge equally necessary to the task. As Walter puts it succinctly to Jesse, 'You teach me the business, and I teach you the chemistry.' Insisting on chemical purity and proper protection, Walter is also sufficiently 'alienated', in Bhabha's terms, to take on board Jesse's experience, namely, that they will need people with enough 'street cred' to sell the product, particularly on the scale Walter has in mind. And the ambivalence or hybridity of Walter remains intact: we soon discover that Walter has decided to turn to a life of crime in order to leave his family a nest egg after his death: he is a saintly 'Cap'n Cook', a drug pusher who, unlike his student, is not merely a criminal but also a martyr. At the same time, he is willing to engage with people of the calibre of the local drug pushers contacted by Jesse, and, as we see in this episode, is willing to kill them to protect himself and his new enterprise. The secular cultural 'contingency' that Bhabha notes is seen when White makes a tape recording for his family. Assuming that he is about to be gunned down by the DEO, Walter assures his family that he loves them and has acted on their behalf. Ironically, he is mistaken about the sirens, as we soon discover.

The ultimate result of Walter's blasphemous hybridity involves both contingency and incommensurability. This episode is framed by Walter, standing before us in his Y-fronts, underwear that from Jesse's point of view only a middle-aged teacher would wear. In the beginning we first see this comically bizarre scene and then the episode retraces the past three weeks in the life of Walter to make clear to us what has happened when we return to the present at the end. The contingent and incommensurate element here is Walter's need to change from his street clothes so that when he returns to his home the smells and stains of the drugs will not give him away. The comic spectacle of Walter in the middle of the desert in his underwear aptly illustrates what Bhabha means by a 'poetics of relocation', a father/chemistry teacher transformed into a criminal/drug producer or drug cook, not to say crook.

Finally, we have the comic incommensurability of Walter, trouserless, pointing his pistol at the oncoming highway traffic in preparation for the police who never arrive. As already mentioned, he expects to be gunned down like a local drug lord. Instead, he discovers that the sirens are those of fire engines, not the police. Walter, the novice hybrid – the erstwhile law-abiding citizen newly introduced into the realm of drug producer/pusher – has assumed that his day of reckoning has come; he has yet to discover that he is one of many in the drug world who remain under the radar. The poignancy and comic, almost farcical quality of Walter lies in his hybridity, his ability to maintain the values of respectability and criminality at the same time, a decent family man reduced to his Y-fronts and a pistol. Moreover, the humour of 'debagged' Walter turns the hybrid balance in his favour; indeed, it would be hard to explain the great popularity of *Breaking Bad*, that seems to have exceeded all sales records for a television series, without recognising Walter as a figure evoking our empathy. In short, the family man turned outlaw for the welfare of his wife and children goes beyond hybridity, leading us to ponder the question, why can't a law-abiding father any longer earn a decent living? The little guy has become the subaltern even though he is as white as his exploitative boss. And we are left to consider, as Bhabha predicted, the secular cultural consequences. Thomas Piketty, a world-renowned French economist, has pointed out that the United States in the past two decades has among the 'advanced' or Western countries the greatest disparity between rich and poor. Indeed, in the past, the USA had, according to Piketty (78), proportionately the largest middle class of any of these countries. Now many Americans like Walter have been pushed down towards a lower class. Blasphemous hybridity is a not only a means of survival for individuals but also signals a cultural change, something well beyond Bhabha's conception.

Hybridity as blasphemy in Sherlock, series 2, episode 1

Bhabha explains that blasphemous hybridity is a form of translation:

> If hybridity is heresy, then to blaspheme is to dream. To dream not the past or the present nor the continuous present; it is not the nostalgic dream of tradition, not the Utopian dream of modern progress; it is

the dream of translation as survival ... an iteration that is not belated, but ironic and insurgent (Bhabha, 324).

Bhabha points out that this particular form of translation emphasises the 'foreignness of translation ... foreground[ing] the "foreignness of cultural translation"' (325). *Sherlock* is a form of cultural translation, not merely another version of the Conan Doyle stories but an 'imitation' of them in the most positive sense of that term, that is, an adaptation of nineteenth-century mystery stories into twenty-first-century police procedurals. Perhaps the best example of the most blasphemous in this series is 'A Scandal in Belgravia'. This episode involves Irene Adler (Lara Pulver), a dominatrix who has acquired access to state secrets from her well-connected clients, one of whom is a member of the royal family. Deeply fascinated by Irene, Sherlock (Benedict Cumberbatch) has even perhaps fallen in love with her. In any event, he saves her life, remaining in contact with her even after the case is concluded. Conan Doyle's confirmed bachelor has been translated into an ironic present of 'insurgent' sexuality.

Moreover, Sherlock, although revered and respected as a brilliant criminal investigator, is subject to an establishment hierarchy that constricts and frustrates him. In addition to the stupidity of the police and the occasional obtuseness of Watson (Martin Freeman), Sherlock is continually annoyed and pestered by the conventions of society and of the Internet, not to mention the disapproval of his prim, prissy brother Mycroft (Mark Gatiss), the royalist mandarin. To satisfy his Twitter fans, or rather those who respond to Watson's blog, Sherlock is obliged to wear the famous deerstalker hat, a relic from Conan Doyle that he clearly detests. And at the Christmas party his detecting habit of sniffing out hidden motives results in his inadvertently exposing Molly's love for him, occasioning one of the rare moments when Sherlock is so embarrassed that he actually apologises to Molly (Louise Breally), stepping well out of character to give her a little peck on the cheek. Moreover, the scene at Buckingham Palace near the beginning of the episode pits Sherlock against the royal family and its representative, Mycroft, who, as Sherlock points out, epitomises their past. The nature of Sherlock's relationship with his brother is made clear when the elder brother remarks, when pouring the tea, 'Shall I be mother?' eliciting Sherlock's reply, 'Therein lies the history of our past.'

Here we see one of the rare moments when Sherlock and Watson laugh together, in particular when Watson realises that Sherlock is naked beneath the sheet, awaiting an audience with a representative of the queen. Sherlock at first resists getting dressed, then refuses to take the case, eventually caving in to authority but not before showing himself to be subversive, not only by his inappropriate dress but also by stealing an ashtray from Buckingham Palace. We recall that upon first arriving, Watson marvelled at the opulence of the palace, adding that he had an overpowering desire to steal an ashtray. However, Sherlock accepts the case not merely as a service to the queen but also because he is intrigued. Instead of blackmailing the queen as Sherlock expects, Irene Adler asks for nothing, simply asserting her power over the most powerful person in the realm. To resolve this problem Sherlock makes use of blasphemous hybridity.

Although Moriarty (Andrew Scott), the traditional villain from Conan Doyle, frames this episode, the focus is upon Irene Adler, his agent, whose weapon, according to Mycroft, using a phrase that is perhaps a high point of royalist euphemisms, is 'recreational scolding'. Mycroft believes that Moriarty has directed Irene to mesmerise Sherlock, thus enabling the villain to sabotage an aeroplane of innocent people. Sherlock focuses upon Irene. Appearing to be a heartless dominatrix, Irene, Sherlock realises, is capable of love covered up by seeming hostility and indifference, resembling his own behaviour. For instance, while Irene extracts her phone from Sherlock by drugging and whipping him, Sherlock is no less violent with the aggressive CIA operative who assaults Mrs Hudson (Una Stubbs), throwing him out of the window more times than he can remember, or so he claims. And, in addition to his cruelty to Molly, previously mentioned, he remarks to some children asking if their dead mother has gone to Heaven, 'People do not go to Heaven, they are put in a little room and burned.' Yet beneath this exterior of calculated toughness of mind, Sherlock and Irene develop an affinity for one another.

And Sherlock solves the riddle of the code of the phone, recognising Irene's desire for him: when holding her hand he feels her elevated pulse and notices her dilated pupils. She in turn appeals to Sherlock by recognising that they share something more than momentary fascination. Irene struggles to survive as a 'misbehaver', as she puts it, and Sherlock, with his 'uncommonwealth' intelligence, as he puts it, is a mental misbehaver constantly hampered and misunderstood by lesser mortals. Blasphemous hybridity is a balance between misbehaviour and self-protection. After all, recreational scolding might be said to be Sherlock's *modus vivendi* as well as that of Irene, although his is verbal and intellectual, for the most part, and hers involves more use of the whip. Each is balanced by their goals, his to solve crimes and hers to satisfy desires. The end, however, involves a final heresy, an imbalance. Sherlock may be in love with a woman who tells Watson that she is gay. And she, whatever her real sexual orientation, loses the game because of love for Sherlock since the passkey to her secrets is SHER. Even Sherlock loses his hybrid balance when he asks Watson for Irene's phone after saving her from execution. Call it virtual and/or unrequited love. Such is a translation of Conan Doyle into a present without nostalgia. Sher falls for a gay dominatrix, or is this an instance of translation of Conan Doyle's Sherlock Holmes into a virtual Sher, a trick of present-day technology? The hybridity of this updated Sherlock involves cultural translation from a late Victorian world to a twenty-first technological post-modern one.

Both *Sherlock* and *Breaking Bad* end with an emphasis on sexuality that gives a particular focus to the blasphemous element of hybridity. At the beginning of the episode when his wife tries to excite him after a harrowing day of difficulties, the worst being the diagnosis of fatal lung cancer, Walter understandably is unable to 'get it up'. At the end of the episode, after perfecting the 'art' of crystal meths and gassing two drug pushers, he presents his wife with a priapic surprise. Similarly, Sherlock seems oblivious and unresponsive to the blandishments of the doting Molly but becomes enamoured by and then deeply attracted to Irene Adler. Sexual potency in both instances is the power to change, for Walter from the pedagogic underling to the drug lord, for Sherlock from Mycroft's view of him, 'What would you know about it [sex]?' to a relationship with a woman his brother regards as beyond the pale and certainly well beyond his little brother. Change of character and change of culture seem to be ideas that receive more emphasis in the films and television programmes than is of interest to Bhabha, who views hybridity as a constant state.

Nonetheless, hybridity is an important cultural idea. A recent television documentary programme on slavery illustrates this point. In a BBC programme entitled *Britain's Forgotten Slaves*, aired on 15 and 22 July 2015, David Olusoga presented a project

he organised at University College, London, to trace the owners of slaves in Britain. The task was facilitated by the Slavery
Compensation Commission, a register of those who were com-
pensated for their slaves as part of the settlement of the Act of
1834 abolishing slavery in Britain. What is little known about this
key historical event is that a vast amount of money was paid to
the slaveholders. Olusoga estimates that in present values it is the
equivalent of about £70 billion paid to over 40,000 British owners of slaves, ranging from a country vicar receiving £800 for one
slave to the father of William Gladstone who was paid the equivalent of £80 million. Needless to say, none of this money was paid
to the slaves. The bulk of this vast fortune was ultimately invested
in the institutions and infrastructure of what makes up present-
day Britain, from the Royal Society and the British Museum to the
Great Western Railroad. Slavery, as Bhabha suggests, underpins
British society, a fact which certainly also applies to European
colonial powers and to the United States. Most tellingly for
Bhabha is the hybridity at the heart of the abolition agreement.
Slaves were no longer to be treated as property, yet billions were
paid to the slave owners to compensate for their loss of property. History demonstrates that the static nature of hybridity is
a significant idea: Britain and most western 'advanced' states are
free, not slave countries. In the modern media, however, hybridity
seems to be of more interest as a means of change, a way of evolv-
ing from one form of hybridity to another, even beyond hybridity. The question this personal development raises is how much
leeway does the society burdened with hybridity permit to the
individual to move beyond it. In the next chapter I shall consider
Pierre Bourdieu's sociological theory focusing on the amount of
individual freedom that is permitted within the perimeters created
by the society as a whole.

5 Pierre Bourdieu and sociological theory

Bourdieu as a sociologist views society as a whole and is interested in the outer limits of culture, the framework for what he calls 'lifestyle'. Three factors are key in Bourdieu's view of the cultural effects upon personality: (1) habitus, explained by way of The Invisible Woman *and* Magic in the Moonlight; *(2) field or human context, seen in* Lincoln *and* Homeland; *(3) lifestyle, examined in* Mr Turner *and* Peaky Blinders.

Literary critics are drawn to the theories of Pierre Bourdieu, Professor at the École des Hautes Études en Sciences Sociales at the Collège de France until his death in 2002, because he radically questions the application to individuals of the deterministic principles of sociology. For Bourdieu, the constants that the social scientist uncovers in the analysis of personal interrelations form only ultimate limitations. Those perimeters, however, allow for various 'lifestyles', the term Bourdieu uses for different individual career pursuits. Although by no means turning his back on the empirical data of his discipline, Bourdieu is ever vigilant to avoid what he calls 'positivist laziness':

> Reflective analysis of the tools of analysis is not an epistemological scruple but an indispensable pre-condition of scientific knowledge of the object. Positivist laziness leads the whole, purely defensive, effort of verification to be focused on the intensity of relationships found, instead of bringing questions to bear on the very conditions of measurement of the relationship … In order to believe in the independence of the 'independent variables' of positivist methodology one has to be unaware that 'explanatory factors' are also 'powers' which are only valid and operative in a certain field (Bourdieu, 87).

Power here refers to the individual who has a choice, however limited, concerning to what extent they accept or abide by the factors in a specific field, a key term for Bourdieu to be taken up in a later section of this chapter. For our present purposes *field* can be taken to mean a specific social context, ranging from a business meeting to a birthday party. Bourdieu's point is that the sociological restrictions upon an individual must be understood as at once internal and external, other-determined and inner-directed. The determining factors that the sociologist finds at the business meeting or the birthday party may be accepted or resisted by any participant: although the resister and accepter will both show the effects of the constraints of the social situation, the result is different behaviour, ultimately difference in lifestyle. For the literary critic interested in the relationship between a character and their social context Bourdieu offers an approach that is not completely deterministic, providing latitude for some free will, some poetic licence.

Bourdieu expresses this position succinctly: 'one only has to realise that the classificatory schemes which underlie agents' practical relationship to their condition and the representation they have of it are themselves the product of that condition, in order to see the limits of this autonomy' (486). Autonomy here refers to an explanatory factor that is taken to be an independent variable, that is, independent of the will of the individual. The freedom of the individual here is, of course, incomplete, constricted by the social situation, which is rendered by the sociologist, according to Bourdieu, in scientific and empirical terms. This limitation of personal development and behaviour is precisely what is taken as a given by the critic analysing literary character. A literary persona seen to be completely determined by the social situation is considered stilted, an automaton. On the other hand, a literary character presented as completely free of social constraint is seen as fantastical, unreal.

Bourdieu devises a formula for understanding how the individual has enough room within the social constraints to express his or her distinctive personality, to develop what he prefers to call lifestyle (Figure 5.1). A literary critic, however, is very unlikely to resort to a diagram like this; for Bourdieu it serves as a sign of his respect for sociological methodology. At the same time, Bourdieu is at pains to demonstrate his understanding that the main complaint of critics against sociologists is that they tend to reduce literary characters

THE HABITUS AND THE SPACE OF LIFE-STYLE

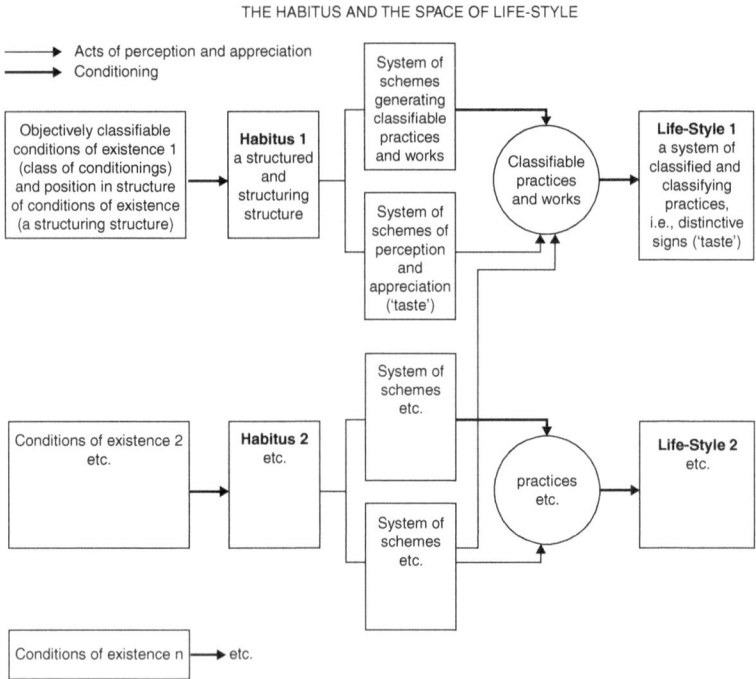

```
──────▶  Acts of perception and appreciation
─────▶  Conditioning
```

| Objectively classifiable conditions of existence 1 (class of conditionings) and position in structure of conditions of existence (a structuring structure) | → | **Habitus 1** a structured and structuring structure | System of schemes generating classifiable practices and works | Classifiable practices and works | **Life-Style 1** a system of classified and classifying practices, i.e., distinctive signs ('taste') |

System of schemes of perception and appreciation ('taste')

| Conditions of existence 2 etc. | **Habitus 2** etc. | System of schemes etc. | practices etc. | **Life-Style 2** etc. |

System of schemes etc.

Conditions of existence n ──▶ etc.

Figure 5.1   Pierre Bourdieu's conditions of existence, habitus and lifestyle.

to agents determined by forces beyond their control, mere puppets. Bourdieu asserts that his theory uses the instruments of his discipline but permits more individual freedom.

This diagram introduces us to the three main principles of Bourdieu's theory: habitus, field, and lifestyle. Habitus will be the subject of the first section of this chapter, the first stage in the diagram above. In the second section, I move on to the middle portion of the diagram above which is referred to as 'systems of schemes' or what, as we shall see, Bourdieu understands as fields. My final section will consider the third and final phase diagrammed above: lifestyle. At the outset it is well to keep in mind that the above diagram begins with an initial state described as follows: 'objectively classified conditions of existence (class of conditionings) and position in structure of conditions of existence (a structuring structure)' (Bourdieu, 167). Bourdieu is here presenting his version of Marxist class or social position with the proviso that the individual's perception of their class status is at once a view of that structure and a contributor to that structure, that is, 'a structuring structure'. This status provides a starting point for the development of habitus that is subject to the force of fields and results in lifestyle.

Habitus: Ralph Fiennes' *The Invisible Woman* (2013) and Woody Allen's *Magic in the Moonlight* (2014)

The term *habitus* combines habit, both in the sense of clothing and customary behaviour or habits, with inhabitant, being at home, at ease with one's mental outlook. Bourdieu describes habitus using the phrase 'the hearth of mental activity' (169), meaning a prevalent way of thinking that is habitual, a predisposition that is not fully conscious, a view of and way of acting in the world that seems natural, as in comfortable, well-worn mental clothes. According to Bourdieu, these habits are formed at a very early stage: the tastes of baby food and colour preferences, family furnishings, the surroundings imbibed by a child all contribute to the formation of the habitus of adulthood.

A term used by earlier sociologists but a focal point for Bourdieu, habitus is at once an individual mode of behaviour, a way of being or acting in the world, and a means of perceiving or understanding the world. The complexity of this position derives from the fact that what we see and comprehend is not merely a function of how we think and respond but also of how we act and behave. What is profoundly sociological in Bourdieu's position is that the social and the solitary, the self and society, are intimately bound together, never separate: Bourdieu offers us a double mirror: the self reflected in the society and the society reflected in the self. Each individual habitus involves different practical actions and develops into different lifestyles:

> The habitus is necessity internalized and converted into a disposition that generates meaningful practices and meaning-giving perceptions; it is a general transposable disposition which carries out a systematic, universal application – beyond the limits of what has been already

learnt – of the necessity inherent in the learning conditions. That is why an agent's whole set of practices ... are both systematic, inasmuch as they are the product of the application of identical (or interchangeable) schemes, and systematically distinct from the practices constituting another life-style (Bourdieu, 166).

Habitus in The Invisible Woman

The Invisible Woman begins with a quotation from Charles Dickens that seems particularly apt for Bourdieu's concept of habitus: 'A wonderful fact to reflect upon, that every human creature is a profound secret and mystery to every other' (*A Tale of Two Cities* 15). Bourdieu would certainly agree with Dickens, even though Bourdieu's subject is actual 'human creatures' and Dickens' is literary characters. Here again we see why literary critics are drawn to Bourdieu's theory. However, *The Invisible Woman* is about the person Dickens (Ralph Fiennes), not a literary character, in particular, his relationship with his mistress, Ellen (Nelly) Ternan, played by Felicity Jones. As one would expect with someone like Dickens who was not only a writer of high repute but also a revered and respected public figure, his life is intimately bound up with his writing. The habitus shared by Nelly and Dickens is that of the theatre and public performance. While Mrs Dickens (Joanna Scanlan) is a stout, dowdy, stay-at-home mother, Nelly is a beautiful young actress who meets Dickens while performing in a play by his friend Wilkie Collins, entitled *The Frozen Deep*. Their friendship, based at first upon mutual friends and an interest in the theatre, finally develops into love. The courtship also involves the theatre or the theatrical; the turning point is when Dickens reads a passage from *Great Expectations* to Nelly:

> You have been in every prospect I have ever seen since – on the river, on the sails of the ships, on the marshes, in the clouds, in the light, in the darkness, in the wind, in the woods, in the sea, in the streets. You have been the embodiment of every graceful fancy that my mind has ever become acquainted with ... Estella, to the last hour of my life, you cannot choose but remain part of my character, part of the little good in me, part of the evil (*Great Expectations* 272).

Drama is doubly present here since Dickens is reading this pas-sage aloud, always with him a performance, and the scene in *Great Expectations* is itself dramatic in that we are presented with the spec-tacle of the ambiguity of love, either a parting of the ways or a new beginning. The power of the scene derives from the equilibrium of the two possibilities, hovering between despair and hope, between, in Wilkie Collins' terms, the frozen deep and a spring thaw. And of course Nelly and Dickens remain between the two in that their love relationship is never made public, never results in marriage.

Dickens' public persona with regard to Nelly is made clear in his declaration in *The Times* that their friendship in no way dis-honours Mrs Dickens. Although we and Dickens' inner circle of friends know this statement to be untrue, Dickens is putting up a respectable front not only for his wife and children but also for himself, his public image. And here we see how the shared habitus of Nelly and Dickens leads to different lifestyles. As Mrs Dickens points out to Nelly, 'You will have to share my husband with his public.' As an actress, Nelly too has her public, but once she decides that Dickens' intentions are honourable – that she is not merely his 'whore' – she seems content to focus upon life with him and let the public think what they will. Dickens, however, is at great pains to maintain an aura of public respectability, symbolised by his building a wall between his bedroom and that of his wife; she cannot share his literary-theatrical habitus.

For purposes of public consumption, Nelly and Dickens are mutual friends, sharing a habitus. Their difference of lifestyles, the family man versus the single actress, helps to preserve the façade of respectability. The scene of the train wreck makes this distinc-tion very clear. After recovering from the initial shock of being thrown out of the train and immediately making certain that Nelly is unharmed, Dickens agrees when she tells him to pretend that he was alone, thus maintaining his image as an honourable man – whose first concern is for Nelly's safety – and a respectable public figure who maintains discretion about his private affairs. Nelly here is demonstrating her understanding of what Mrs Dickens had pre-dicted, that Dickens is wedded not only to the women in his life but also to his public.

This difference in lifestyle is made emphatic at the end of the film. Six years after Dickens' death in 1870, Nelly marries George

Wharton Robinson who remains unaware that his wife was Dickens' mistress. He is presumably one member of the public for whom Dickens maintained his image of public respectability. By contrast, the local vicar, the Reverend Benham, senses that Nelly has a secret that she needs to confess, an eventual confession that presumably becomes the source of the information in the film. We are left to assume that now that Dickens is dead Nelly feels she can confide in the reverend about her past life with the great writer. The distinction – the title of Bourdieu's most famous book and, as we shall see, the goal of lifestyles – between the ends of the lives of these two lovers is stark. Dickens dies a man divided from himself, unable to ever make public his love for Nelly, while Nelly finally confesses her secret, leading, we may assume in the film, to general public knowledge of the affair. Following Bourdieu's model, this distinction – a word he chose carefully – is the result of a difference in lifestyle. In conclusion, Nelly seems now to be retired from the stage, having married into a very comfortable upper-middle-class rural squirearchy that is remote from the literary theatrics of Wilkie Collins and Charles Dickens. Perhaps. Or have the social conventions changed from the middle of the nineteenth century to the 1870s when what was in Dickens' day scandalous has now become less shocking and more intriguing? Does history preside over the development of habitus towards various lifestyles?

Habitus in Magic in the Moonlight
The second example of habitus is chosen because it demonstrates how a single habitus can lead to opposite lifestyles, in this instance, in the same person. The main character, world-famous magician, Wei Ling Soo, Stanley to his friends, played by Colin Firth, is also well known for unmasking false spiritualists. His habitus is therefore that of a sceptical, rational, pessimistic non-believer. When his old friend Howard Burkan (Simon McBurney) offers him the challenge of unmasking a new clairvoyant and mystic, Sophie (Emma Stone), he responds with his usual sublime confidence in his reasoned, detective-like ability to see through deception. At the beginning of the film, Stanley is completely without self-doubt; as a magician he is very successful at deception and has yet to meet anyone whose attempt at deception he cannot explain in rational terms. He fervently believes there are no tricks he cannot himself reproduce.

Sophie, however, seems to be more skilful than any of his previous conquests. Not only is she continually able to make reference to details of her clients' lives that she could not have known by any rational or empirical means, but, unlike Stanley, she makes little of her ability, wearing it lightly as something she was born with, not a great talent or wondrous ability. Instead of putting herself forward as a spiritualist, she shows an interest in Stanley and asks him continually why he is interested in her. He contends that she is an impostor whom he wishes to demonstrate to be a fraud. When Sophie shows knowledge of the past love relationship of his Aunt Vanessa (Eileen Atkins), the woman who raised him, he becomes convinced that Sophie is a true medium. Now he does an about-face, becoming a follower and admirer of Sophie as a clairvoyant. What is interesting for us at this point is that Stanley shows the same personality pattern, the same habitus, as a believer that he did as a sceptic. He is now as certain of Sophie's ability as he was before of his own ability to unmask all false irrational forms of deception, including that of Sophie. He even goes so far as to call a press conference to confess his conversion and to laud the spiritualism of Sophie. At this point, Stanley demonstrates that the habitus is a mental propensity, a way of approaching, acting in and understanding the world, but the lifestyle that results from that viewpoint depends not merely on the habitus but the context or field, to be considered in our next section.

The film is, however, complicated by another factor, the love angle. Sophie has fallen in love with Stanley but finds that with all of his hard-earned admiration for her ability as a medium he is unaware of her love and of her as a love object. When she asks if he has any personal interest in her, he is taken aback. After all, he points out, she is much younger than him and engaged to marry someone else, a suitable young man who is deeply in love with her and very wealthy. This subplot is interrupted when Vanessa has a life-threatening car accident. Aunt Vanessa, we recall, is Stanley's surrogate parent, the source, in Bourdieu's terms, of the initial elements of his habitus. In fact, Stanley is so desperate to save Vanessa that he resorts to prayer. He finds that his new believing lifestyle has limits; he cannot pray, even for his beloved aunt. In short he comes to understand the outermost limits of his habitus and the 'habitual' scepticism returns. Pretending to vanish from the room, he remains in a chair unseen overhearing Sophie and Howard speak of their deception of Stanley. At first he is angry and hurt but then he comes to admire their cleverness, recognising that they have taken a string from his bow.

He now returns to Aunt Vanessa uneasy and unhappy. Very adroitly and indirectly, she leads him to admit that he is in love with Sophie; the home of the habitus has a special power over him or, as Bourdieu would suggest, the person who helped form his habitus can help redirect it. Now Stanley proposes to Sophie, but his abrupt, rational, forthright manner – his habitus – is anything but romantic. Sophie is put off by his egotistical offer of himself as a great prize, leaving him with little hope. However, in the end she comes to prefer him to her rich boyfriend. Sophie has been forced to choose between two extreme forms of habitus, one overly romantic and sentimental and the other too rational and distant. We infer that she realises her boyfriend, like Shakespeare's Duke Orsino, is in love with love. Stanley in his own strange way/habitus loves her. Some have found this conclusion hokey and contrived. Perhaps it is. For our purposes it could suggest that Sophie has come to terms with Stanley's habitus and recognises that he has done his best in a realm unfamiliar to him, that of romance. In fact, I suspect that if most of our spouses did not make allowances for the romantic limits of our habitus we would still be single. I know I would. *Magic in the Moonlight* shows us that although the habitus can result in opposite lifestyles it still is subject to ultimate limitations and that is why for Bourdieu it is a habitus. However, the film adds a new dimension to habitus: is it possible that becoming conscious of the limits of our habitus, as in the case of Stanley, can enable us to change lifestyles?

Field or social space: Steven Spielberg's *Lincoln* (2012) and Howard Gordon and Alex Gansa's *Homeland* (2011)

The field or social space is for Bourdieu the context that makes habitus important, leading to results that he calls practices. Habitus could simply be reduced to taste but for its effects in a cultural field or space:

> The dispositions which govern choices between the goods of legitimate culture cannot be fully understood unless they are reintegrated

into the system of dispositions, unless 'culture' in the restricted nor-
mative sense of ordinary usage, is reinserted into 'culture' in the
broad anthropological sense and the elaborated taste for the most
refined objects is brought back into relation with elementary taste for
the flavours of food (Bourdieu, 93).

Culture in the limited sense of a visit to a museum must be brought
back into the larger sense of culture as a whole, ranging from museums to football games. For it is in this broader context, according to Bourdieu, that habitus has a significant effect and is itself
effected and formed. The result of the interchange is what he calls
practice:

> Because it can only account for practices by bringing to light the
> series of effects which underline them, analysis initially conceals the
> structure of the life-style characteristic of an agent or class of agents,
> that is, the unity hidden under the diversity and multiplicity of the
> set of practices performed in fields governed by different logics and
> therefore inducing different forms of realization, in accordance with
> the formula: (habitus) (capital) + field = practice (Bourdieu, 95).

Capital will form part of the lifestyle to be analysed in the next section of this chapter. Here we need only understand that the habitus in
a field results in practices, a term that includes actions and thoughts
that are manifest in the culture, that have social consequences.

The fields, for Bourdieu, are various and varied but must be seen
to function like dialects or regional languages – and here the influence of Saussure is obvious – as dynamic interactional systems.

> There are thus as many fields of preferences as there are fields of sty-
> listic possibles. Each of these worlds – drinks (mineral waters, wines,
> or aperitifs), or automobiles, newspapers, or holiday resorts, design
> of house or furnishing of house or garden, not to mention politi-
> cal programmes – provides the small number of distinctive features
> which, functioning as a system of differences, differential deviations,
> allow the most fundamental social differences to be expressed almost
> as completely as through the most refined and expressive systems
> available in the legitimate arts; and it can be seen that the total field of
> these fields offers well-nigh inexhaustible possibilities for the pursuit
> of distinction (Bourdieu, 223).

Distinction for Bourdieu is not an objective, quantifiable entity, like a certificate of merit; instead it involves acceptance of a desired place in the social hierarchy:

> However contrary to theories of the autonomy of the world of ideas or of 'objective knowledge without a knowing subject and subject-less processes' (in which Louis Althusser and Karl Popper concur), it has to be pointed out that objectified cultural capital only exists and subsists in and through the struggles of which the fields of cultural production (the artistic field, the scientific field etc.) and, beyond them, the field of the social classes, are the site, struggles in which the agents wield strengths and obtain profits proportionate to their mastery of this objectified capital, in other words, their internalized capital (Bourdieu, 225).

These fields, perhaps more accurately characterised as cultural battlefields, are indeed locations of hierarchical strife, competitions ranging from economic survival to social prestige. And Bourdieu insists that high culture – the quiet, pensive social spaces of learning, such as museums, libraries, and laboratories – are sites of violent competition.

> Cultural objects, with their subtle hierarchy, are predisposed to mark the stages and degrees of the initiatory progress which defines the enterprise of culture ... like Christian's progress toward the heavenly Jerusalem ... Hence the incessant revisions, reinterpretations, and rediscoveries which the learned of all religions of the book perform on their canonical texts: since the levels of 'reading' designate hierarchies of readers, it is necessary and sufficient to change the hierarchy of readings in order to overturn the hierarchy of readers (Bourdieu, 226).

The social hierarchy presents a challenge to the new entrant. Triumph is also defeat for once the entrant unlocks the secret of entry to the higher level, the key is then available to others. So to protect the prestige of this level of the hierarchy the key must be changed, overturning the hierarchy of readers. Yet total secrecy can never be maintained lest the quest becomes futile and appears only open to the favoured few. The process of protecting and opening up the hierarchy, ascending the ladder and replacing it with another, is continuous. Hierarchical societies – and only the most remote and small are without hierarchies – are battlefields.

The field in Lincoln

Lincoln is a film that focuses upon the violent cultural field of congressional politics in order to produce a very practical result, the passage of the thirteenth amendment to the US Constitution freeing the slaves. Although entitled *Lincoln*, the film concerns the last few months of Lincoln's life, from January to April 1865, when he was killed at Ford's Theatre. The Civil War is nearly over; the Confederacy has clearly been defeated. Lincoln, however, is anxious to have the anti-slavery amendment adopted because even though his Emancipation Proclamation of 1863 freed the slaves, questions about its permanence and legality will be raised after the war. Moreover, after the Confederacy surrenders and re-enters the Union, most of the representatives from those states that seceded from the Union will vote against the amendment. So the only possibility of passage in the legislature will be in the few months before the Civil War comes to a formal conclusion.

The field for Lincoln's habitus as well as that of the others involved is as violently competitive as Bourdieu would have us expect. The stakes are high for all concerned, not the least being the slaves themselves. Everyone has something personal at stake; the issue is not completely intellectual for anyone, including Lincoln. Fields have an effect on the resulting practice of the habitus because they reach into the very core of our being, leading to decisions that not only compromise our principles but are heart-wrenching, threatening our sense of stability and selfhood.

In order to pass the amendment freeing the slaves Lincoln has to contend with the two extreme factions of his own party as well as attracting some from the opposition Democratic Party. For Lincoln there are two immediate problems. The 'horse-trading' must be completed quickly before the official surrender of the Confederacy that would bring into the legislature much more opposition. In addition, as president he must remain above the fray, his integrity unquestioned both for his personal self-respect and so that he can continue to be seen as the leader. The obstacles always involve the clash of habitus, which the film reminds us continually is much more than a clash of ideologies – although that is certainly a factor – but also involves personal and pragmatic matters.

Even the most overtly ideological and idealistic of the legislators have personal issues. On the Republican side, Lincoln contends
with the conservative Francis Blair (Hal Holbrook) who feels that
ending the war and preventing more bloodshed is more important
than freeing the slaves, a position that becomes immediately understandable when we learn that his two sons are in the army. On
the other hand, the leftist Republicans led by Thaddeus Stevens
(Tommy Lee Jones) want not merely an end to slavery but also total
equality, that is, voting and interracial marital rights. Stevens' high
principles come down to earth when we see him going to bed with
his black servant, treating her as if she were his legal wife. The film
shows very skilfully that both politicians are men of principle even
though their principles are intimately bound up with their lifestyle,
to employ Bourdieu's term.

The behaviour of those in the Democratic Party is less overtly
ideological or principled since most of them are minor figures, lame
ducks soon to be out of office. Lincoln bristles at the idea of brib-
ing these people; as an alternative, he suggests offers of 'patronage', government positions appointed by the president, in return for
votes. All one can say of this strategy is that, like the Emancipation
Proclamation, it achieves the goal even if the means are questionable ethically if not legally. So the poor Democratic losers struggle no
less than the president with their consciences versus their economic
needs and political ambitions. It is an all-too-accurate rendering of
the Washington political battlefield then and now.

Yet the film adroitly avoids cynicism. Daniel Day-Lewis' portrayal
of Lincoln certainly helps in this regard. Whether he is speaking to
the fighting black soldiers or the marginal men hired to hand out
patronage jobs for votes, or to his son and wife, Lincoln has a modest
dignity, a profound intelligence that is without arrogance, and a deep
and abiding love for his country and its people. Although he stands
out above all others as a homespun prophet of his time, others also
rise to the challenge of history. And it should never be forgotten that
Lincoln's Achilles heel, his connection to the rest of us mortals, is the
dilemma of his son Todd. A very patriotic young man, Todd wants
desperately to join the army. Lincoln tries to stop him, knowing that
his wife, who is still recovering from the death of another son, will
be utterly devastated if Todd is lost, not to mention his own agony.
So he must send other people's sons to the slaughter and prevent his

own from going with them. The point is not that Lincoln is to blame; who shall remain blameless if attempting to prevent the destruction of our family is a crime? Rather, the point is that Lincoln, perhaps the greatest US president, is human, one of us: that is probably the secret of how he got elected. And the burden of not being able to send his son into his war weighs on him every day.

Another historical figure rising to prominence in this film is Thaddeus Stevens, who is certainly the finest intelligence of the legislators. Arguing masterfully for full equality for the black man, he exposes the blind prejudices of his colleagues with blistering wit and highly contemptuous comedy. And in the end he is taunted by them for compromising; instead of insisting on full equality he votes with Lincoln, telling a white lie, that he only believed in equality before the law, not full equality. Stevens is discerning enough to realise that at that time full equality would never be supported by the majority either in the legislature or the country. Freeing the slaves is a first step, and he follows Lincoln, whom he admires for his adept leadership and assessment of what can be accomplished at the time. Yet no two men could be further apart from one another in terms of personality. Habitus involves difference, not necessarily contradiction or opposition. Indeed, the passing of the thirteenth amendment could be said to be the fruit of the battle of the habitus. Democracy can only proceed if there is compromise on the battlefield of habitus.

The film ends with the death of Lincoln, one of the greatest tragedies in the history of the United States. We see Tad Lincoln, the youngest son, at a children's theatre enjoying an adventure drama that has just concluded with a sword fight to the death, presumably for the bad guy; suddenly, an actor interrupts announcing that the president has been shot. First we see Tad desperately holding onto the theatre balcony as if it were his father followed by the woeful sight of Mrs Lincoln. In one sense we have been prepared for this death. At Petersburg, the last great battle of the war, Lincoln is seen on horseback surveying the corpses, himself almost as grey and lifeless as the bodies on the ground. After the surrender at Appomattox Court House, Lincoln sits in a rocking chair on the front porch with General Grant. True to his habitus, Lincoln asserts that mercy not hanging must be the order of the day, particularly for the soldiers, who should be allowed to return to their families as soon as possible. Even with regard to the leaders the president shows malice towards none; he wishes they could quietly slip away out of the country. The commander-in-chief of the Union forces of the Civil War is sickened by war – Grant remarks that Lincoln has aged ten years – but is thrust into the field of civil strife that becomes a battlefield because he fervently believes slavery is wrong in the eyes of God. Yet Lincoln is remembered and revered not as a war president but as one who saved the Union because his habitus could only be thrust into war by a field that offered no other viable alternative.

For our purposes, we can remain with Lincoln during the war, a vivid example of Bourdieu's habitus in a field. The film points out that in Lincoln's last speech – and it is his first public reference to the matter – he refers to the principle of the black man's right to vote. Spielberg is here making clear that had Lincoln lived he would not have be satisfied merely with emancipation: total equality for black people was Lincoln's goal, an end that gives further justification to his prolongation of the war to secure passage of the thirteenth amendment. The film thus raises Lincoln above his context or field, but Bourdieu suggests that one field only gives way to another, that we must always be subject to the ultimate limitations of a field. Lincoln is so revered that the film seeks to raise him above all of that: how successfully is another question.

Nonetheless, the field that Lincoln struggles through in order to pass the thirteenth amendment illustrates how Bourdieu's field differs from, say, the context of daily life. The field that mediates between habitus and lifestyle is one of fierce personal competition involving the social hierarchy. From his own Republican party, Lincoln faces opposition on both the right and left wings; he skilfully manoeuvres between these two extremes, promising Blair to listen to the Confederates who wish to agree on a cessation of hostilities and making clear to Stevens that freeing the slaves is but the first step towards total equality. The problem Lincoln must confront is personal and social. Stevens is a man of principle and can be convinced by logic and political savvy. Blair must be placated; Lincoln sends a delegation to meet with the Confederates, as he promised, but does not allow them to negotiate or come to Washington lest the other representatives believe that the war is about to end. The social dilemma involves, as Bourdieu would have predicted, hierarchy; Lincoln is the head of the Republicans, but he owes to these two highly placed members of his party his position of leadership, so Stevens must be convinced and Blair must at the very least not be alienated. Is it any wonder that, as Lincoln says to Grant near the end, he feels a weariness in his bones, a moment when he looks so like the image of him at the Washington memorial. In short, the ordeal that the Lincoln habitus has endured in the field has produced the lifestyle that makes him one of the greatest men of US history.

The field in Homeland, series 1, episode 1

The field in *Homeland* is the complex and intriguing one of counter-terrorism. Carrie Mathison (Claire Danes) has been sent back by the CIA to Washington after she conducted an unauthorised operation in Iraq. During that operation a prisoner, in exchange for saving the lives of his family, told her that a US prisoner had been 'turned' by Abu Nazir, a senior al-Qaeda operative. Upon her arrival back in the United States, she is summoned to a meeting in which her superior announces that Delta Force has just freed a US marine who has been held captive for eight years. He is about to return home to a hero's welcome; Carrie suspects that he is the prisoner who was turned and is planning some sort of terrorist attack in the United States.

Carrie wishes to place the marine, Nicholas Brody (Damian Lewis), under surveillance, a near impossibility – he is about to be given a medal by the vice-president for his courage and cannot be treated as a suspect – as her immediate superior, Saul Berenson (Mandy Patinkin) points out. Moreover, Saul's superior, David Estes (David Harewood), has little time for Carrie whom he regards as a loose cannon misguidedly indulged by Saul. In addition to the hierarchical problems as a lowly case-worker on probation, Carrie also has personal difficulties. Berenson and Estes take a very different approach to counterterrorism and have diametrically opposed views of Carrie. In addition, Carrie suffers from a serious psychological condition that requires daily medication, which explains her obsessive dedication to her job, what we might call her habitus.

With the help of Saul and against Estes' wishes, Carrie is allowed to be present at the debriefing of Brody. She asks some very telling questions that Brody does not answer satisfactorily, further fuelling her suspicion but also reinforcing Estes' disapproval of her obsessive approach – her habitus. Carrie remains undeterred. Without Saul's approval she arranges for one of her friends at the agency to set up a surveillance system on Brody that feeds not into the CIA but into her own home. Visiting her house, Saul discovers the system, is extremely angry, telling her to get a lawyer. She responds by making obvious sexual moves, saying isn't there anything she can do to make things up between them. Incandescent with rage, Saul replies, 'What the fuck are you doing?'

So now Carrie has made major mistakes in both personal and hierarchical terms; she has alienated her mentor, Saul Berenson, the man who first hired her, and has now lost the protection of the CIA. How does a very obsessive habitus get through this minefield? Drowning her sorrows at a bar, she notices Brody on television at various public appearances making peculiar moves with his fingers that are repeated at each public event. Convincing Saul that these finger movements may be some kind of coded message that Brody is sending back to Abu Nazir, he approves her clandestine surveillance project. We thus are introduced in this first episode to the lifestyle of the main female character of *Homeland*. Her entire life is devoted to counterterrorism; who else would have noticed the finger movements of Brody after she believed herself to be fired from the CIA and without the protection of her mentor? We also understand that to become a CIA operative and to survive at the bottom of the food chain, obsessive paranoia is the modus operandi. Such is Carrie's field, one for which we might all need her medication. Later in the series, we will discover that Carrie is correct; Brody is indeed planning to kill the vice-president. And we are left to ponder whether Carrie's personality is the result of the field in which she lives and works or if it is her habitus that draws her to such a world. Bourdieu's diagram placing habitus before field may be merely an abstract way of rendering a process that is intermingled or may be in need of modification.

Lifestyle: Mike Leigh's *Mr Turner* (2014) and Otto Bathurst's *Peaky Blinders*, series 1, episode 1 (2013)

Bourdieu's concept of lifestyle combines personal disposition, individual psychology, with social class or prestige, what he calls 'cultural capital'. The central thesis of Bourdieu's *Distinction* focuses upon lifestyle:

> If it is true, as I have endeavoured to establish, that, first, the dom-
> inant class constitutes a relatively autonomous space whose struc-
> ture is defined by the distribution of economic and cultural capital
> among its members ... to which there corresponds a certain life-style,
> through the mediation of the habitus; that, second, the distribution
> of these two types of capital ... is symmetrically and inversely struc-
> tured, and that third, the different inherited asset structures ... com-
> mand the habitus and the systematic choices it produces in all areas
> of practice, of which the areas commonly regarded as aesthetic are
> one dimension – then these structures should be found in the space of
> life-styles (Bourdieu, 257).

According to Bourdieu, all lifestyles are subject to the market forces
of economic and cultural capital. Those in the aesthetic field who
profess 'disinterest' in this tawdry monetary and social world are
nonetheless bound by it; the attempt of the artist or critic to transcend this world is itself testament to its universal prevalence:

> Because they are opposed to those producers who offer products
> directly adjusted to the dominant taste, ... those writers and artists ...
> are the predestined bearers of the eschatological hopes which, inso-
> far as they support their 'inner-worldly asceticism' and their sense of
> 'mission', are the true opium of the intellectuals. The analogy with
> religion is not artificial: in each case the most indubitable transcend-
> ence with respect to strictly temporal interest springs from the imma-
> nence of struggles of interest (Bourdieu, 317).

Opium is here a clear reference to Marx, who referred to religion
as the opiate of the masses. Bourdieu suggests that for the bour-
geoisie the opiate is art. The artistic perspective 'above' this battlefield of economic and cultural forces only reinforces its unavoidable
power, yet Bourdieu is not dismissing the mission of aesthetic ascet-
icism. Rather, his point is that the artist must have enough money
to survive and enough cultural prestige so that their art will be
seen, heard, or read. The content of art may well deserve respect
for questioning the very forces that enable it to exist. The artist,
usually of the middle class, is no less subject to primal necessities
than those of the lowest class. And it is not sufficient for the artist to
put him or herself in the position of the lower class, say by working

in a factory (presumably temporarily), because the habitus of the 'worker' involves more than merely the economic factor.

> It is not a question of the insupportable image of the working-class world that the intellectual produces when putting himself in the place of a worker without having the habitus of a worker, he apprehends the working-class condition through schemes of perception and appreciation which are not those that the members of the working class themselves use to apprehend it (Bourdieu, 373).

To understand the dilemma of the working-class worker one must for Bourdieu take into account not merely the economic context but also the socio-psychological factor, the habitus. Again, Bourdieu's point is not to dismiss opposition but to emphasise that any attempt to question or subvert the status quo is based upon the reality of the status quo: 'It tends to be forgotten that the specific logic of cultural dominance means that the fullest recognition of cultural legitimacy can and often does coexist with the most radical challenging of political legitimacy' (Bourdieu, 396). But, Bourdieu insists, the political context affects everyone, artists included. In a discussion of the utopian world of Marx and Engels, where anyone can become an artist, Bourdieu points out that by imagining a social world in which 'anyone in whom there is a potential Raphael' of painting or politics could develop without hindrance, it forces one to see that the concentration of the embodied or objectified instruments of production is scarcely less in politics than in art, and prevents one forgetting all the potential Raphaels whom the mechanisms responsible for this monopoly keep excluded much more effectively than any 'ideological state apparatuses' (Bourdieu, 398).

For Bourdieu, this notion of how potential talent and ability are hindered by the socio-political context is not merely a philosophical position but a form of practical knowledge accepted by the man in the street. The evidence Bourdieu offers for this general knowledge is an empirical analysis of abstentionism, the refusal to answer the political questions of pollsters, representing the average person's belief that the political system lacks any means for or interest in forwarding their potential. 'Abstentionism is not so much a hiccup in the system as one of the conditions of its functioning as a misrecognised – and therefore as a recognised – restriction on political participation' (Bourdieu, 399).

In fact, Bourdieu believes that there is a general and widespread apathy and disillusionment with politics deriving from the manner in which the establishment surveys the people while avoiding their point of view and then disseminates the results, a form of misinformation by way of language that is regarded as a sham. Yet this general scepticism at the same time represents an acceptance and at least tacit understanding of the power of the establishment.

> Everything combines to reinforce the deep distrust – not incompatible with an equally deep form of recognition – which the dominated feel toward political language, broadly identified, like everything symbolic, with the dominant, the masters of the art of packaging and of fobbing off with words. This suspicion of the political 'stage', a 'theatre' whose rules are not understood and which leaves ordinary taste with a sense of helplessness is often the source of 'apathy' and of a generalized distrust of all forms of speech and spokesmen. And often the only escape from ambivalence or indeterminacy toward language is to fall back on what one **can** appreciate, the body rather than words, substance rather than form, an honest face rather than a smooth tongue (Bourdieu, 467).

Lifestyle in Mr Turner

This final phrase provides an apt introduction to *Mr Turner*. The opening scene of the film presents Turner (Timothy Spall) as a bodily presence, a sprawling, awkwardly eccentric figure dressed more like a beggar than a painter, making his way impatiently on bowed and bandy legs beneath a body emitting incomprehensible gestures, abruptly slamming his way into his house, uttering his first word, 'Oy!' Whether or not the face is honest remains to be determined – as indeed it will be – but it is safe to assume from his demeanour that he has no time for common pleasantries or idle banter. Turner is introduced to us by showing not how he paints or looks at the scenes of his painting but by how he behaves in his quotidian existence, how he acts in the world familiar to him. In short, *Mr Turner* begins with a walking definition of Bourdieu's lifestyle.

And what a strange lifestyle it is. While unpacking his purchases of pigments, his maid, addressed as Damsel (Dorothy Atkinson), wafer thin and covered in psoriasis, lurks asking awkward questions, some of which are ignored, some answered curtly, and a few courteously. Next enters Turner's father (Paul Jesson), greeting him more as a housemate than a son. Their conversation – consisting primarily of an interchange of guffaws and grunts – refers to the now long-dead wife/mother who is regarded as both a saint and a bitch. Welcome to the home of 'Billy' Turner. The accent of the few phrases that pass between them indicates a working-class origin now overlaid with a more sophisticated vocabulary and the occasional middle-class twang. The house, clearly well beyond the means of the working class, even if sparsely and strangely furnished (not surprisingly), suggests that Turner is a successful painter, a man, in Bourdieu's terms, of considerable cultural capital.

For our purposes, the film can be seen as an interpretation of Turner's lifestyle. The habitus is that of a man in a man's world whose person and house show no sign of a woman's touch, with the exception of the occasional animal-like sex with the maid while both remain fully dressed. Yet Turner is clearly loved by his father and, as we gradually learn, by his maid. In his eccentric way, Turner is a decent man, demonstrating very real charity to Hayden, a ne'er-do-well painter and fellow student at the Royal Academy, whom the other members of Royal Academy regard as an ungrateful scrounger not worthy of charity. Turner, however, loans him fifty pounds, a large sum in those days, and later forgives the debt owed to him by Hayden, who, true to his lifestyle, remains ungrateful.

As Bourdieu would have predicted, Turner's habitus began at an early stage when he first painted pictures that were hung in his father's barber shop; it would seem at that stage he acquired a taste – an important term of Bourdieu's – for landscape and seascape, neither of which had in his day the prestige or cultural capital of portraits. Turner accepts with good humour his place in the outer showrooms of the Royal Society, not in the main rooms where Reynolds and Gainsborough are displayed. And he remains as unmoved when his pictures come into fashion as when they go out again. For Turner, landscapes and seascapes are his milieu, neither better nor worse than any other. When Ruskin preciously announces his preference for Turner's vibrant pictures over Claude Lorrain's static views, Turner defends Claude as good of his kind. Turner seems to sense that his choice of subject matter for his painting is a function of his habitus, derived possibly from the primal scene of his father's barber shop, where in those days he would have witnessed everything from surgery to wig-making, a very mundane world of physical human needs. The brute physicality of Turner's work is brought home to us in the scene where he insists on having himself lashed to the mast of a ship during a storm in order, we presume, to paint such a scene realistically. Not surprisingly, his finest seascapes, those presenting a violent unforgiving view of the sea, an eerie beauty untamed by domestic harmony, offended Queen Victoria. Another habitus, another lifestyle, another era.

How does such a man become a great painter, one whose work presents not only the external beauty of landscapes but also the full range of emotions that involve a response to and understanding of the external world? The explanation is the love relationship with Mrs Booth, a respectable woman who develops a deep love for Turner. Interestingly, for nearly the last twenty years of his life, Turner lives with her in her home under an assumed name. The habitus develops an alternative lifestyle, and accordingly he treats Mrs Booth with affectionate respect, quite unlike his attitude to his maid. It would appear that Mrs Booth represents the woman he longed for and never found in his mother and that much of his gruffness was a defence mechanism, a form of deep disappointment. Yet after his death the maid mourns for him no less than Mrs Booth, as if each loved a different man. Does this suggest that Mr Turner as presented in the film was a man of more than a single habitus?

Lifestyle in Peaky Blinders, *series 1, episode 1*

The title *Peaky Blinders* refers to the peaked caps that were rumoured to contain a razor blade, a required and distinctive part of the dress code that included matching smart and well-cut suits of this Birmingham gang of the 1920s. The hat functions as a sign of their lifestyle, suggesting that the traditional cloth cap of the worker, the subservient, is quite the opposite, now stylish, subversive and presumably armed. In the opening scene when Tommy Shelby (Cillian Murphy) on horseback summons the Chinese woman to cast a spell on the horse to win the next race, the entire community is riveted by the spectacle, betting on the horse, as Tommy predicted. The overt signs of the gangster lifestyle are crucial to his 'street cred', his cultural capital. Here, the strategy is to convert cultural capital into economic capital; he lures the punters in until the stakes are high enough to make it worth his while to turn on them, raking in a huge profit. Actually this scene begins with the Chinese 'sorceress' who has been summoned by Tommy on behalf of the Peaky Blinders to cast a spell on the horse. The family, terrified, anxiously sends off the young woman to do the bidding of the gang, whatever it may be. The point is that the Peaky Blinders rule the neighbourhood; there can be no appeal to the police, who must obviously be on the take.

Clearly this series is a British equivalent of the US series, to be analysed in Chapter 6, *Boardwalk Empire*. While the habitus of the American gang relates to the corruption that pervades the entire society, including all ranks of law enforcement, the Peaky Blinders derive theirs from the First World War. Even the British police-man, C. I. Campbell (Sam Neill) recognises that the gang members are patriots who served courageously in the war. And poor shell-shocked Danny 'Whizz-Bang' Owen (Samuel Edward-Cook) makes clear, periodically 'running amok', the effects of the war, particu-larly of the artillery. Another war veteran, Freddie (Iddo Goldberg), Tommy's mate from the front, addresses the local factory work-ers as a communist, making clear why they share contempt for the establishment. First he asks how many were soldiers in the war, wit-nessing the death and wounding of their comrades. Most raise their hands. Then he asks who profited from the war, the soldiers or the officers. Replying with them, he states that their reward is to have their pay lowered. He then takes a strike vote that is unanimous. The British workers recognise that they have been exploited as can-non fodder by their superiors who, in this episode, are represented by no less than Winston Churchill, a Conservative government min-ister who instructs Campbell to bury the bodies deep enough to keep them out of the newspapers.

The class dilemma of *Peaky Blinders* leads to a parting of the ways between Tommy and his friend and battle-mate Freddie. Instead of a life on the wrong side of the law, Freddie takes up the political battle. Yet the friends are both disillusioned with the estab-lishment even if it takes each of them in different directions, a vivid example of how a similar habitus can lead to various and quite dif-ferent lifestyles. Most of the Peaky Blinders are adamantly opposed to communists and other leftists who are unpatriotic subverters of the free enterprise system that is so skilfully exploited by the gang in their lucrative backroom bookie business. For Inspector Campbell, the policeman sent in by the government, this attitude is useful in his assignment from Churchill to stop the support among the left; he hopes to enlist the help of the gang against the communists and the Fenians.

Tommy, however, is in a peculiar position. His gang has inadvertently stolen guns – the gang were apparently drunk and mistook the gun boxes for motorcycle parts – that the government was selling to Libya, another scandalous 'body' the Conservatives do not want to reach the newspapers. Furthermore, Tommy, the thinker of the gang, is wary of Campbell as someone who observed, that is, was in the reserve at home, never on the front experiencing active combat in the war. The matter is further complicated by the fact that Freddie, the communist, is romantically involved with a woman who is related to the ruling family of the Peaky Blinders, the gang that is adamantly opposed to communists. The choice between political and illegal subversion is ever present for the working class. When Freddie and Tommy talk about it at the local pub, Tommy suggests that they both offer false hope to the poor but occasionally his horses win, the implication being that Freddie is backing a losing horse. Again, a similarity of habitus, bred in war, and a similar field, post-war gangland Birmingham of 1919, can lead to different lifestyles.

Mediating between the gang, the government and the communists and Fenians of the left, Tommy manages to develop from a peaky blinder habitus into a unique lifestyle that is made clear at the end of this episode. In one of his fits of panic, Danny has killed an Italian who threatened him with a knife. Unfortunately, the victim is a member of a rival gang that demands retribution. As Tommy explains, he must be the executioner of Danny to prevent the Italians doing it their way, which involves emasculating him then letting him bleed to death. After securing promises from Tommy to look after his wife and children and not to bury him in the mud – the location of the artillery that, as he explains, has driven God from his soul and destroyed his mind – Danny shakes hands and obeys his 'sergeant major'. Danny's respect for Tommy derives in part from the fact that Tommy received two medals for valour and clearly was admired by the men under his command. The brilliantly theatrical false execution – the use of a bullet full of sheep's blood that stuns rather kills Danny and the boat to transport the body to prevent a police investigation – convinces the Italians that Danny is dead while he, unaware of the plan, is in fact only immobilised by shock. Later, awakening unharmed on a canal boat taking him out of Birmingham and away from the watchful Italian gang, Danny first wonders if he is in Heaven until the boatman points out that his presence as a member of the gang precludes the possibility of Heaven. Instead, he goes on to explain that the shock is intended to awaken Danny from his obsession with the war and that in return for saving his life Tommy has a little job for him in London. Danny has been recruited into the Peaky Blinders, and we are shown how Tommy is shrewd enough to outmanoeuvre both the Italian gang and Inspector Campbell, the government man.

Formed by a habitus largely hardened by war – as is made clear by his addiction to opium and his frequent violent dreams of battle – Tommy returns home after the war to develop a lifestyle adapted to a lawless city, a sort of civic minefield, particularly for the working class. As the barmaid who is Campbell's spy, Grace Burgess (Annabelle Wallis) points out, the real leader of the Peaky Blinders is not Arthur, the titular leader, but Tommy, the brains of the outfit. For the world of Birmingham after the First World War is far more complex than Arthur can understand. And we see that Grace and Tommy share an insight that sets them apart: Tommy's only remark to her in this episode is to ask her if she is a whore and to warn her that if not she shouldn't be there.

In that brief moment we start to see an entirely new sort of lifestyle for Tommy. Could he ever join with Grace, cross class and political lines, even break the mould of his habitus? The word in the pub is that since returning from the front Tommy is not interested in women, but that is not the impression he gives us when he stares at Grace. Or, are these two forever on opposite sides of the battlefield, she the daughter of a policeman executed by the IRA and he the working-class soldier psychologically ruined by war? Freddie, who shared Tommy's field of battle, has been able to adopt a lifestyle that includes romance, but, as Bourdieu would remind us, the possibility of a similar lifestyle for Tommy is dependent upon outward circumstances and inner choice. At the conclusion of this episode, Tommy has gone back on his promise to the leaders of the gang to return the guns to the government by leaving them in a prominent place where they will be found. Instead, he decides to keep them since the government in its desperation to find them has 'shown their hand', indicating their value. Tommy will exact a price for the guns and we can but wonder whether he may thereby have eliminated an alternative lifestyle for himself. Moreover, Tommy, as his sister points out to him, is making an ethical choice for himself and his gang: they are now gun-runners, enemies of the government, that is, not in political opposition like Freddie's communism but at a new level of criminality. Does this choice represent a change of lifestyle for Tommy, a move that most of the other gang leaders, including Tommy's own family, would consider dangerously unethical? Unlike Bourdieu, the end of this episode suggests that ethical decisions may result in a change of lifestyle. In the next chapter, Martha Nussbaum considers the question of ethics in a cultural context.

6 Martha Nussbaum: ethics and literary theory

Nussbaum begins by analysing the limitations of the two preva-
lent ethical theories, those of Kant and Bentham. My analysis of
My Week with Marilyn *and* Downton Abbey *serves to clarify this*
argument. The alternative Nussbaum recommends involves: (1) an
interpretation, with the emphasis on 'an' rather than 'the', as
exemplified in the discussion of The Artist *and* Boardwalk
Empire; *(2) feelings and correct judgement in relation to* The Help
and Weeds.

Martha Nussbaum, Ernst Freund Distinguished Service Professor
of Law and Ethics at the University of Chicago, begins her 1989
essay 'Perceptive Equilibrium: Literary Theory and Ethical Theory'
by pointing out that literary theory shows an interest in many forms
of philosophy but, most notably not in ethics. She hopes to promote
what she calls a 'joining' of the two disciplines:

> I imagine, instead, a future in which our talk about literature will
> return increasingly to a concern with the practical – to the ethical
> and social questions that give literature its high importance in our
> lives … A future in which … a literary-philosophical inquiry will
> ask what literary works express … in terms of 'content' but also,
> and inseparably, in virtue of their forms and structures, their ways
> of describing … In short, a future in which literary theory (while not
> forgetting its many other pursuits) will also join with ethical theory
> in pursuit of the question: 'How should one live' (Cohen, *Future* 58).

Nussbaum reiterates the above position in the introduction to the
volume, entitled *Love's Knowledge* (1992), going on to point out
that while focusing upon the novel she does not consider her ideas

as applying only to that genre: 'Not only novels prove appropriate, because ... many serious dramas will be pertinent as well, and some biographies and histories ... I leave for a future inquiry as well, the ethical role of comedy and satire, both in the novel itself and in other genres' (Nussbaum, 46). By extension, I shall argue that film analysis – particularly if considered as a visual form of narrative, comedy and satire – can also facilitate the 'join' between literary theory and ethics. This chapter will focus on three of Nussbaum's ideas about the relationship between literary theory and ethics:

1. Literary analysis provides an alternative to the two most preva-lent philosophical ethical positions, Immanuel Kant's moral duty and Jeremy Bentham's utilitarian morality.
2. Unlike these prevalent philosophical views, literary analysis is based upon the holistic principle of coherence, what might be called a comprehensive interpretation, with emphasis on 'a' rather than 'the'.
3. Literary analysis leads to a belief that 'feelings may after all in many cases be an invaluable guide to correct judgement; that general and universal formulations may be inadequate to the complexity of particular situations, that immersed particular judgements may have a moral value that reflective and general judgments cannot capture' (Nussbaum, 73).

An alternative to Kant and Bentham: Simon Curtis's *My Week with Marilyn* (2011) and Julian Fellowes' *Downton Abbey*, series 6, episode 5 (2015)

Nussbaum begins by pointing out

the sense that we are social beings puzzling out, in times of great moral difficulty, what might be for us the best way to live – this sense of practical importance, which animates contemporary ethical theory and has always animated much of great literature, is absent from the writing of our leading literary theorists (60–1).

Here we see at once the innovative and classical elements of Nussbaum's thinking: innovative in her opposition to the literary-theory establishment and classical in her adoption of Aristotle's concept of ethics. For those of us not conversant with Aristotle's ethics, Nussbaum explains as follows:

> As Aristotle observed … great literature … is deep and conducive to our inquiry about how to live because it does not simply (as history does) record that this or that happened, it searches for patterns of possibility – of choice, and circumstance, and the interaction between choice and circumstance – that turn up in human lives with such persistence that they must be regarded as our possibilities (Nussbaum, 171).

Instead of pursuing Aristotle's ethics for further clarification, I suggest we follow the lead of Nussbaum, who proceeds by distinguishing Aristotle – or, more accurately, Nussbaum's version of Aristotelian ethics – from those of Kant and Bentham, particularly as her ethical procedure usually involves a decision not about what to do but about what not to do. Nussbaum defines her inquiry as seeking 'what is it for a human being to live well' and explains that this pursuit is both empirical and practical (59–62). It is empirical in being based upon actual human experience, not, as Kant believed, *a priori*, and practical in that the inquiry is not 'pure', detached, and abstract but a search for what can be done in our lives. In these ways, Nussbaum distinguishes her view from that of Kantian moral duty and Bentham utilitarian ethics:

> 'How should I live?' This choice of starting point is significant. This question does not (like the Kantian question, 'What is my moral duty?') assume that there is a sphere of 'moral' values that can be separated off from all the other practical values that figure in a human life. Nor does it assume, as does the Utilitarian's focus on the question, 'How shall I maximize utility?' that the value of all choices and actions is to be assessed in terms of a certain sort of consequence that they tend to promote (Nussbaum, 173).

An alternative to Kant and Bentham: My Week with Marilyn
I begin with *My Week with Marilyn* because in addition to raising moral and ethical questions it is clearly a cultural document and is, in Nussbaum's terms, empirical. The film derives from the actual

diary of an event that occurred in 1956 when Marilyn Monroe came to England to make a film with Sir Laurence Olivier entitled *The Prince and the Showgirl*. The young man appointed to look after her while abroad, Colin Clark, wrote an account of his experience which formed the basis of the film. And at that time Marilyn Monroe was a cultural phenomenon as famous in Hollywood as Olivier was on the London stage. Since Nussbaum emphasises that her kind of ethics accounts for us as social beings not merely morally dutiful or sage utilitarians, this cultural meeting between Hollywood and the Old Vic is a social event directly related to morality and ethics, particularly as it was much debated at the time whether Olivier was compromising his artistic reputation and whether Marilyn risked tarnishing her image by sharing a double billing with him. In Nussbaum's terms the film has clear practical consequences.

It would indeed be very difficult to apply the notions of moral duty or utilitarianism to Marilyn Monroe as presented in this film. In fact, her daily behaviour contradicts both. As an actress she is unable to remember her lines and seldom arrives at rehearsals on time. From the point of view of moral duty she is wasting the time of people of the stature of Dame Sybil Thorndike (Judi Dench) and Sir Laurence Olivier (Kenneth Branagh), to mention but two, who are far beyond her in the realm of theatre and acting in general. And even if we consider the utilitarian defence, as adopted by her acting coach, Paula Strasberg (Zoë Wanamaker), that a great budding genius needs time and understanding, we are not convinced, mainly because Marilyn makes quite clear that she does not believe herself to be a great talent. Moreover, further to her moral discredit, after Arthur Miller has left her alone in London, she flirts shamelessly with Colin (Eddie Redmayne), many years her junior, in front of his girlfriend who is thus made aware of what is happening.

So what do we make of Marilyn as portrayed in this film? Can we dismiss her as a 'sex goddess', the overindulged object of Hollywood hype? At one point, Olivier in exasperation encourages her to be just that, 'just be sexy'. Insulted, Marilyn stalks off the set. So we have to admit that she wants to be an actress, whatever we may think of her attempts. Moreover, the appeal of Marilyn seems to go beyond mere sexiness; surely there were women at the time who equalled or exceeded her good looks and figure. Even Olivier himself admits in an unguarded moment how natural and beguiling she is on film. And although the young, inexperienced Colin is mesmerised by her, he is not merely sexually attracted to her. After all, he lies beside her in bed for an entire night without attempting anything physical. Proudly announcing that he has fallen in love, he confesses at the end that she has broken his heart 'a little bit'. Women also respond to Marilyn, sensing something more than physical attractiveness. Dame Sybil Thorndike points out to her that she is incomparable as a film actress, and Vivien Leigh (Julia Ormond), Olivier's wife, notices how her husband gazes almost trance-like at the film rushes, in which Marilyn lights up the screen.

Trying to define Marilyn's appeal is likely to result in defining our own limitations. It is important to indicate what she is not, that is, merely a sex object. Those satisfied with that definition could then apply moral and utilitarian criteria to condemn her as an unprofessional because not properly utilising her physical attributes and as morally corrupt, a married woman toying with young Colin. The unique quality of Marilyn is difficult to isolate. Moving aside the moments of histrionic petulance when she turns to her acting coach, seemingly unaware of anyone else except herself, we need to focus on her at her best, most pointedly, for example, at the end when before leaving for home she stops at the local pub where Colin is staying to say goodbye and to thank him, remarking to the publican, 'a nice place you have here'. But for this final gesture we might have thought that she took Colin for granted. Similarly, at the final scene of the movie, she apologises to the cast and staff, forcing us to reconsider her unprofessional behaviour. Her audience at the pub and at the studio (which of course includes us) is rapt, almost bewitched by a strangely beautiful candour that is characteristic of Marilyn. No one else in the film could have made that remark to the publican.

When she is relaxed before an audience that she feels is responding positively to her, or even when she dances seductively unaware that she is being recorded, she has an almost ineffable charm. During this dancing scene even the camera crew is totally enthralled with Marilyn, not because she is a brilliant dancer (which she is not) but by virtue of her ability to fascinate and hold our attention, a movie director's dream actress. And the studio bosses fall over themselves with the thought that if she has this effect on the crew of professionals, who, above all others we would expect to be immune to such charm, what a draw she will be for the general audience. Moreover, instead of the huge ego one would expect of such a star, she is desperately fragile, crestfallen at Arthur Miller's comic version of her and stunned when Dame Sybil refers to her achievement as a movie actress. In short, if you respond positively to Michelle Williams' rendition of Marilyn, you share some of Colin's love. And advocates of moral duty and of utilitarian ethics can but shrug their shoulders. For Nussbaum, love's knowledge goes beyond the sphere of these old ethical categories. Art alone in its various forms can point the way to this alternative. The Marilyn of this film – no matter how far from the 'real' Marilyn – is an artistic character that arouses enough of our interest, if not love, to render the moral imperatives of duty and utility irrelevant.

The key moment for Colin is when Marilyn summons him to her residence refusing to carry on with the film or see anyone else. Here Colin treats her honestly, calms her down, and ends up sleeping in bed beside her for the night. They spend the next day together sightseeing in London, enjoying one another's company. By the third day she seems to recover, announcing to Colin that she wishes to put aside all that has happened between them, returning to the set. We are left in doubt as to whether this fling is merely a part of the regular routine of Marilyn's professional life when she periodically needs personal reassurance and companionship, enabling her to face the demanding professional life as a glamour queen. Or was she for a moment really in love with Colin? We will never know, and it is probable that neither Marilyn nor Colin will either. The ethical question is complicated here because Marilyn, knowing that Colin has an ongoing relationship with the wardrobe assistant, Lucy (Emma Watson), deliberately toys with Colin in front of her, causing the end of that relationship.

The film suggests that Marilyn's personality is so bound up with charming men (and many women) that she is not capable of making morally dutiful or even utilitarian choices about when to use or pursue this ability. Her alluring lights are always on except when she is asleep and perhaps even then as well. So we are left with either some form of moral or utilitarian disapproval – she is an evil woman or does not make proper use of her talent – or a willingness to empathise with a woman who is almost wholly without self-esteem and yet has the ability to charm almost everyone who lays eyes on her. Heartbroken at the end, Colin seems to have achieved love's knowledge, admitting with a mixture of joy and sadness that he is one of the many unable to avoid succumbing to the temptation not only of her beauty but of her continual need to be reminded of the power of her attraction, not just by a husband or occasional lover but also apparently almost every day by a different person. The ethics of love's knowledge alone brings us to understand that the source of Marilyn's charm is to be so disarmingly unable to believe in her capacity to charm that she needs reassurance every day, resulting in series of broken hearts, like that of Colin. In the end, the film moves beyond Nussbaum's love's knowledge in suggesting that even if after empathising with her problem you condemn Marilyn in ethical terms you still have to be impressed by her ability to offer an alluring and charming image on the screen.

An alternative to Kant and Bentham: Downton Abbey, *series 6, episode 5*

This particular episode of *Downton Abbey* caused quite a stir because the climax is Lord Grantham (Hugh Bonneville) at the dinner table in what appears to be his death throes, spitting up blood. One reviewer quipped that he thought he was watching not *Downton Abbey* but *Alien*. The episode is particularly embarrassing since Neville Chamberlain (Rupert Frazer) has been invited as the guest of honour. And his presence is related to the ethical problem of this episode. Violet Crawley (Maggie Smith) invited Chamberlain, in his capacity as minister of health, to help in her campaign against reorganisation of the local hospital. Cora, Lady Grantham (Elizabeth McGovern), and Lady Mary (Michelle Dockery) are in this matter opposed to Violet. So the family conflict is between preserving the past and modern improvement. Lord Grantham's dramatic collapse renders that matter moot. In short, all parties to the debate about the hospital place their love of Lord Grantham above their difference of opinion about the hospital. And, of course, it is not coincidental that the cause of this radical change of priorities is medical. The ethics of love prevails over that of the moral duty to preserve tradition and the utility of modernisation in that the public debate at the table about the hospital ceases when Lord Grantham's health is in danger.

The powers and dilemmas of love are the organising principle of this episode. Bleeding and lying on the floor, his life threatened, Lord Grantham exclaims to his wife, 'I have loved you very, very much' while she, now a devoted nurse, replies practically and empirically, 'Not your time', determined to save him. She recognises that her love at this moment requires the empirical and practical: stop the bleeding and call the ambulance to take him to the hospital – interestingly, the subject of the debate. The point seems to be that the hospital itself and the service it offers are more important than the specifics as to whether it is to be modernised or to remain rather traditional. To the relief of everyone in the household, Lord Grantham does survive, but the process of his operation, hospitalisation, and convalescence shows how much he is loved by those at Downton Abbey who do not usually express such personal feelings. As Mrs Patmore the cook (Lesley Nicol), points out, Carson, the butler (Jim Carter), who is usually formal and undemonstrative, is clearly shaken. His respect for his lordship has always been apparent but his fondness for the man has not before been expressed. And the redoubtable Countess Violet Crawley shows more concern for her son than about the entire hospital campaign that she organised with the help, she had hoped, of Minister Chamberlain. She admits to having been shocked, having gone into the dining room ready to do battle in the tradition of Wellington and Marlborough. Clearly, Violet can become so concerned about preserving the past that her deep care for her family recedes to the background. Even Barrow (Robert James-Collier), who usually seems cold and calculating – and has had his differences with the head of the household – discovers to his surprise how much he cares about his employer. Instead of pursuing how this emergency relates to the need for a new hospital, the episode focuses on love in the community at all levels.

The subject becomes the travails of love, from Lady Mary discussing with Tom Branson (Allen Leech) the problem of 'marrying down' to Mrs Hughes (Phyllis Logan) coming to terms with Carson's requirements for his meals, further examples of empirical, practical ethical issues that are based upon love rather than mere duty or utility. In both instances, the matter-of-fact conversation covers up very deep emotions. Lady Mary is really deciding who she loves enough, in spite of class differences, to commit herself to for the rest of her life. And Mrs Hughes is clearly trying to work out how to make her husband Carson happy in a new situation without the host of servants that as head butler he has come to take for granted.

One of the most striking illustrations of love's knowledge concerns the defence of the Countess by her maid Denker (Sue Johnston). Dr Clarkson (David Robb) has at the last minute changed sides and taken up with the modernisers of the hospital. Seeing him in the village, Denker confronts him with his betrayal of her mistress and is told by the doctor that she has not heard the last of this matter. The doctor then writes to the countess complaining of Denker's disrespectful treatment of him. Upon hearing from Denker that she did confront the doctor on this matter, the countess informs her that she has no right to any opinion on the matter and should not, in any event, have spoken in such terms to someone above her station. The countess concludes by ordering Denker to leave the house the next morning. When Denker protests that she was only acting out of loyalty to her mistress, the countess replies that she shall then have a 'tepid' recommendation. Denker, however, cleverly inveigles Spratt (Jeremy Swift), the butler whom the countess respects – threatening to reveal that in the past he harboured in the house a cousin who was wanted by the police – into prevailing on the countess to reconsider. Finally, she relents, deciding to keep Denker as her maid. Of course, the means used to defend Denker would not meet the approval of moral Kantians or Benthamite utilitarians.

Even the countess might disapprove if she knew how Denker influenced Spratt's decision. Then we learn at the end of the episode that she is in no position to criticise Denker. When asked about being inveigled into coming to Downton, Neville Chamberlain reveals that he too was blackmailed. As a young man, he helped his brother in a sort of prank that proved to be very serious. They dug a trench across Piccadilly, holding up traffic throughout southern England, not something that, as minister of health, he would want generally known. As Nussbaum had predicted, the justification for what amounts to a form of blackmail is love in a pragmatic situation, that is, the countess deserved to have her position on the hospital heard and duly considered, and Denker, as the doctor himself admitted, deserved to be reprimanded, as she was, but not, in his words, to be beheaded.

Meanwhile, below stairs, Barrow and Molesley (Kevin Doyle), who were anything but friends, reach a sort of entente when Barrow agrees to teach Molesley how to read. From a moral point of view we cannot be certain of Barrow's motivation, but the practical and empirical facts are that Molesley must learn how to read to further his ambition to be a gardener. Even in a place as traditional and old-fashioned as Downton Abbey, the morality of duty and utility is simply not adequate. The needs and desires of the people on all levels of the household require the knowledge of love, knowledge that often involves compromising on matters of stern morality and strictly reasoned utility. In the conclusion of this episode, we see the two sides of the upper class. On the one hand, the entire household rallies around Lord Grantham for his decency, loyalty, and sense of responsibility. On the other hand, the hierarchy is very inflexible for those beneath his level. Denker nearly loses her position for loyally defending her mistress to someone above her station, while her outraged upper-class mistress is able with impunity to blackmail a minister of state. Ethics in this world varies with class status.

A comprehensive interpretation, with emphasis on 'a' rather than 'the': Michel Hazanavicius' *The Artist* (2011) and Terence Winter's *Boardwalk Empire*, season 3, episode 1 (2012)

Nussbaum emphasises that the joining of ethics and literature requires attending to the structural and generic aspects of the literature, not merely to the content: her discussion shows a clear understanding of the principles of literary interpretation.

> We grasp the practical content of a literary text adequately only when we attentively study the forms in which it is embodied and expressed; and … we have not correctly described the literary form of say, a James novel if we have not asked what sense of life it expresses (Cohen, *Future* 62).

The basis of the relationship between literature and ethics for Nussbaum involves interpretation not only of the ethical and moral issues in the text but also of the formal means by which literature presents these issues. The process of literary interpretation of ethical matters is described by Nussbaum as involving what she calls 'perceptive equilibrium': 'an equilibrium in which concrete perceptions 'hang beautifully together' both with one another and with the agent's general principles, an equilibrium that is always ready to reconstitute in response to the new' (Cohen, *Future* 73). Here Nussbaum is pointing to the interpretive reading process that seeks coherence but is ever open to the text revising, even undermining our assumptions as we attempt to understand what has happen*ed* with an openness to what is happen*ing*, that is, the unfolding of the text.

> For stories cultivate our ability to see and care for particulars not as
> representatives of a law, but as what they themselves are: to respond
> vigorously with senses and emotions before the new; to care deeply
> about chance happenings in the world, rather than to fortify our-
> selves against them; to wait for the outcome, and to be bewildered –
> to wait and float and be actively passive (Cohen, *Future* 75).

The active passivity described above involves the attempt to grasp
but not impose order, to remain flexible enough to change and revise
in the face of new and bewildering textual events, that is, events in
the reading process that question our working assumptions, events
that should be seen not merely as frustrating, thwarting our wish
for coherence, but also as welcome challenges, inviting a new interpretation or modification of what we had up to that point taken to
be comprehensive. Once again, instead of pursuing these abstrac-
tions, let us turn to specific examples where these ideas become in
Nussbaum's terms empirical and particular.

Interpretation in The Artist
Set in the Hollywood of the 1920s, *The Artist* is a story about two
performing artists, an older male star of silent films, George Valentin
(Jean Dujardin), and a young star of the new talkies, Peppy Miller
(Bérénice Bejo). Peppy, an extra, happens to bump into Valentin,
the star of the film, on the set of a silent film. Both sensing a kind
of rapport as performers, they begin an improvised dance revealing how naturally they respond to one another as dancers. Deeply
impressed by Peppy's spontaneous performance, Valentin insists
that his boss, Al Zimmer (John Goodman) hire her to do a film
with him. Soon Peppy achieves equal billing with Valentin, but in
1929 talkies replace silent films. Peppy takes to the new medium.
Valentin, however, carries on with silent films, losing his position
at the studio, eventually resorting to declaring bankruptcy and auc-
tioning off his personal effects.

Although Valentin now camps out in a shabby rented flat with
only his chauffeur, Clifton (James Cromwell), and his faithful dog,
Jack (Uggie), Peppy, even at the height of her fame, never loses
interest in Valentin. In fact, by way of an agent, she buys all of his
personal effects, storing them in a room of her house. When, in
desperation, Valentin attempts to commit suicide, she insists that he
convalesce at her home. Upon his recovery, she threatens to leave

the studio unless Valentin is hired to star with her in a new film. The film ends with their tap dancing together to the sound of music – now, of course, a part of the film. The final scene concludes with the only words spoken by Valentin who, we now realise upon hearing his voice for the first time, has a pronounced French accent and could therefore only have small parts and never be a star of the talkies.

The relationship between Peppy and Valentin requires interpretation related to an ethical issue. When they first meet it is clear that there is a considerable age gap between them. Valentin is an established name, married and very well off. Peppy is much younger, single, a novice at Hollywood. Even after she makes her name we see her with numerous male admirers whom she refers to as 'toys'. What is the nature of her feeling for Valentin and, of course, his for her? After Valentin has left the studio their meetings are cordial, somewhat nostalgic. If there is love between them it seems to be that of dancing partners who long to perform together but who now are immersed in different media. Peppy seems to feel a sense of loyalty to Valentin for giving her a break, one that results in her becoming a star, and is upset that he has been cast off rather callously by the studio. At the same time, she recognises that the future lies in talkies, remaining determined to continue with the new medium. Here, the title *The Artist* helps us understand that shared artistry is the real bond between Peppy and Valentin.

Although not suited to talkies, Valentin nonetheless inspires loyalty among his followers. Even when cast off by the studios, Valentin shares his small, shabby residence with Jack the dog and Clifton the chauffeur, who both remain loyal. Indeed, the one negative moment between Peppy and Valentin occurs at the restaurant when, unaware of Valentin being within hearing, Peppy states to a radio interviewer that silent movies need to step aside and make room for the new medium. Angry and hurt, Valentin exits dramatically and abruptly, remarking to Peppy that he is making room for her. Peppy is mortified, unaware until that moment of his presence at the restaurant and meaning no ill will to him personally. In fact, Peppy is always loyal to Valentin. Discovering that she has bought all of his personal effects he attempts suicide, assuming that her purchases served to further her desire to move him out of her way. After taking him into her home, she explains while he convalesces that she only wanted to help him, saving everything as a sort of memorial to him. And, as we have seen, she demonstrates her loyalty by insisting that he be hired back by the studio to do a film with her.

I therefore think that the film is more holistically viewed, to use Nussbaum's term, as less about love and more about loyalty, or at least only love in the form of loyalty. Of course, it is possible that one of the reasons for his divorce is his wife's jealousy of Peppy, but there is no evidence in the film to support that suspicion. This point is reinforced by Clifton and Jack. Jack from early on is part of Valentin's act, responding to his every gesture and, as the policeman remarks who drags him out of the fire, he would not be alive but for the dog. Similarly, Clifton is happy to go on working for Valentin even though he has not been paid in a year. When finally he is forced to leave – because Valentin cannot let him continue working without receiving a salary – he becomes Peppy's chauffeur, later pointing out to Valentin how much he respects Peppy, reinforcing our awareness of her loyalty.

The ethical question that arises in the context of Hollywood stardom is very clear. How can rivals be loyal to one another? How can they be friends in such a fiercely competitive environment? Of course, Peppy has no choice but to replace Valentin when talkies arrive: the larger forces of life, of their environment, ranging from the stock market crash of 1929 to the introduction of voice to film at about the same time, are well beyond the control of any individual. That does not prevent you helping those in more need than yourself even if those in need might misinterpret the charity as a form of condescension. At the end of the film, Peppy helps Valentin out of gratitude for what he did for her at the beginning of her career and because of her respect for him as an artist. The difference is instructive. When at the beginning of the film he insisted that she dance with him in the next film he could hardly envisage that she would soon succeed him as a star. Now at the end when he dances with her, he is unlikely to equal her status let alone surpass it because of his strong French accent. So ethics is often not about changing the world but about quotidian moments in our lives, small acts of friendship and loyalty. All we can say is that Peppy brings a smile back to the face of Valentin. That is the love of Nussbaum's *Love's Knowledge*, at least one form of it. The fond smiles between them in the final dance are less of love than of love of dancing together. *The Artist* ends with the artists dancing together, suggesting that, beyond any ethical issue involving Peppy's gratitude to him for her first break, these artists have an innate understanding of one another, rather like the instinctive understanding between Valentin and his devoted canine, Jack.

Interpretation in Boardwalk Empire, *season 3, episode 1*
This episode opens with a brutal scene involving a relatively small-time bootlegger, Gyp Rosetti (Bobby Cannavale), whose fleet of cars transporting bootleg spirits has been delayed by a flat tyre. A passer-by stops to help, provides some oil, and suggests how to loosen the lug on the wheel to replace the tyre on the rim. Upon first arriving and seeing the men struggling with the rusty lug, he says he has some 'three in one'. Unfamiliar with the phrase, Gyp asks what it is, and the man replies, 'Oil, of course.' After the lug has been loosened with the oil, Gyp defends himself, explaining he is from Sicily where oil usually refers to olive oil. Sensing some aggression, the man explains, 'I didn't mean anything by it', turning back to his car. Gyp then attacks him from behind with a tyre iron, beating the poor man to death, presumably as a sign of power for his followers. Gyp feels that he has been shown up before his men as a foreigner who has not mastered the American vernacular. The episode is full of foreigners, Italian, Irish, and Jewish immigrants among others, who work for the gang. The crime world provided one of the few enterprises of American life in the 1920s that were willing to hire immigrants, many of whom had little alternative but to become the soldiers in the wars among the various groups of gangsters, most of whom were divided according to their country of origin. The so-called melting pot is really a seething cauldron tolerating illegal activities like the bootleg booze trade.

The next scene, focusing on the big boss Nucky (Steve Buscemi), serves a similar purpose but is presented in a different style. A thief who has stolen from one of Nucky's warehouses is tied to a chair. Handed a cup of coffee by one of his underlings, Nucky lectures the manager of the warehouse for his negligence. The thief who steals is only doing his job, but the warehouse manager who does not lock his door is the real culprit. Turning to the thief, Nucky explains that he is not angry with him since he is only doing his job. When the thief has relaxed, Nucky casually asks who was his accomplice. Now that he has the name of the other thief, Nucky reiterates that he is not angry. As the thief heartily thanks him, Nucky instructs his henchman to untie the thief but not before you 'put a bullet in his head'. In the next scene, Nucky is ordering the execution of the accomplice, whose immediate boss, a Jewish immigrant, asks in return a favour of Nucky. After agreeing, Nucky orders his execution as well. We are thus introduced to two forms of gangster violence, a show of power, by Gyp, a small-time mobster, and criminal or gangster justice administered by Nucky, the big boss. Gyp is flexing his muscles, defending his 'street cred' as a new immigrant tough guy; Nucky is saying you may be a thief but you cannot steal from me because no one invades my turf with impunity. Since Nucky was part of and now pays off those in the legal establishment of Atlantic City, New Jersey, the setting of this series, it is quite clear that justice is in the hands of the mob.

By contrast, the life of a law-abiding citizen in this world is seen in the episode involving the door-to-door salesman competing to sell the most irons but being rebuffed at every door he darkens. Finally he wanders into a florist shop where two mobsters are threatening the owner with extortion. Quick-witted, the florist tells the salesman to keep his mouth shut, refers to him as his brother and threatens the mobsters with what is in the salesman's showcase, which in shape and size could well accommodate a tommy gun or sawn-off shotgun. When the mobsters have retreated, the florist rewards his surprised saviour with an order for two dozen irons and a bouquet of flowers for his wife. Delighted, the salesman returns to his supply house believing that he has won the contest, only to be told that he is too late. The contest ended at nine, not ten as he had been told. Clearly, the contest had been fixed so that he could not win, even though, as he explains to his boss who appears to be almost as crooked as Nucky, he planned to buy a house with the winnings. Defeated and dejected, the salesman returns to his dingy rented room where his adoring wife cuddles their infant. When he informs her that he has lost the contest, she gently expresses, in a distinctly foreign accent, the hope that next year he will win. We can be forgiven for not sharing her hope. Lawlessness or rule by those who have power and money – the two seem almost synonymous – is found on all levels of this society. As the scene involving Nucky and the state and federal officials makes clear, the members of the establishment hold him in contempt but accept his money and shield him from the law, such as it is. Moreover, a large portion of the population shares in Nucky's ill-gotten gains. At the party, the dwarfs bring out a treasure chest of little goodies for everyone, and, as they all dig in, one woman remarks, 'They are real diamonds.' Corruption is widespread and involves many people of the upper and middle classes.

It would be a misreading of this episode to assume that the only law is that of the gun. The women reveal a side of the society where ethics has some bearing. Even the head of the brothel exacts a fine from her employees if they drink too much, a law she enforces for their own protection: as she points out, men will only behave properly if women insist that they do so, and drunken women are in no position to insist upon anything. The point is not that women are more ethical than men. One need only think of Nucky's mistress, Billy Kent (Meg Chambers Steedle), to dispel that illusion. She faces Nucky's wife and child without the least sign of regret or chagrin. Rather, some women occasionally succeed in involving their gangster lovers and husbands in a licit element of society. That they do not always succeed is seen in the scene of the death of Manny (William Forsythe). To honour him for being a loyal and loving husband, his wife gives him a new hat. Pleased, Manny dons the homburg, kisses his wife, opens the door and is gunned down. His wife is left with bullet holes in her husband and his new hat. So much for the immigrant's hopes for the promised land.

Nucky's wife Margaret (Kelly Macdonald) is, however, more successful. Having donated some of her own land to be used for the local hospital, she has involuntarily immersed Nucky in the world of philanthropy. It involves complications he had not anticipated. While at the hospital Margaret witnesses a miscarriage that one of the attending doctors explains could have been avoided if the women were taught what foods to avoid while pregnant. Later at her Christmas 'shindig' Margaret approaches the head doctor about this matter; he is defensive and expresses his embarrassment to Nucky. Afterwards, Nucky is angry with Margaret for speaking of business matters and embarrassing a guest at their party. Margaret stands up to him, pointing out that he is pleased to be known as one of the benefactors of the hospital. In short, Margaret is part of the façade of respectability that Nucky needs, and it therefore seems likely that if she chooses to pursue this matter she could prevail.

Margaret's ethical leverage with Nucky derives from her appearance of respectability as the wife of a 'businessman/gangster': hardly an exemplar of moral duty, she houses criminals, witnessing their activities, not something that would win the hearts of utilitarians or Kantians. The ethics of Nussbaum suggests empathy for Margaret and her situation: if she turns on Nucky she may endanger the future of her philanthropic projects, not to mention imperilling the life of her child. Given that context, we can understand her limited attempts at caring for others in a world where the life of another is as dispensable as the life of the passer-by brutally murdered by Gyp or the thief summarily executed by Nucky. Of course, it is possible to see Margaret's behaviour as hypocrisy, a mere semblance of decency and respectability. That is a matter of interpretation, the element Nussbaum insists must be a part of her ethic. And the question then is does the concept of hypocrisy or the ethics of female charity provide a more comprehensive view of this episode.

In this respect, it is well to remember that a woman literally flies above this episode. Carrie Duncan began her attempt at a transcontinental flight from Cape May on 1 January 1923. At the end of the episode, Margaret rushes down to the beach to see her fly overhead, and earlier in the episode comments are made about her flight, the most memorable being that of Nucky: instead of flying, 'she should open her legs and spread her wings for her husband'. Unfortunately, Ms Duncan dies when the plane crashes mysteriously before reaching its destination. Her attempt is clearly an inspiration to Margaret and many others.

The best ethical defence for Margaret's response to the dilemma of the woman who miscarried out of ignorance about proper diet is that of the Talmud: anyone who saves the life of another saves the whole world. Care for another is the essence of ethics, for that is unmistakably the path towards a good life. Nucky sees Carrie Duncan as a woman who is neglecting her place in the social hierarchy, but, as an adulterer, in addition to his other crimes, he is hardly the one to judge her. Margaret sees Duncan as someone trying to exceed the arbitrary limitations placed on women. Even if it fails, an attempt like that of Margaret to educate pregnant women is far more worthy than anything Nucky ever contemplates. For women, ethics in this world presents a choice between the lifestyles of Nucky's wife and his mistress. At least Margaret tries within her own strict limitations to do some good to others in need. And even if she does eventually succumb to the admiration of the young man so enamoured of her, she has struggled to avoid what Billie Kent welcomes literally with open arms and a bare breast. It is perhaps not coincidental that interpretive ethics focuses upon Peppy and Margaret, the women with a sense of decency; one advantage of the 1920s is that women were so completely excluded from positions of power that they could form their own private realms – Peppy's home and Margaret's hospital charity – that become havens for something more ethical precisely because neglected by the male power-brokers.

Finally, it might be useful to compare *Boardwalk Empire* and *Peaky Blinders*, the American and British versions of gangster life in the 1920s. *Peaky Blinders* results from the dreadful conditions of the soldiers in the First World War and their callous treatment by many of the officers; the British gang arises and thrives because of the exploitation of the workers, an extension of what the soldiers in the trenches endured. *Boardwalk Empire* stems from corruption, particularly of legal institutions and law enforcement. For instance, Winston Churchill, unlike his counterpart in the United States, is not 'on the take': he simply has no interest in the workers, who are not likely to share his Tory political persuasions. As in *Downton Abbey*, those in the lower class, the constituency of the Peaky Blinders, have little claim to ethics. Their counterpart in the United States resides, then and now, in a more dangerous place where their lives, not merely their legal rights, are in peril because the police and local politicians are beholden to the mob. Ethics is not a possibility for the bottom feeders of the gang or the 'working stiff'. Interestingly, in both series the women, who are so marginalised from the machismo world of gangs that they create their own subculture, provide new ethical possibilities. Although they represent mere glimpses of an alternative lifestyle, it is important that they point to ethics as the way out of self-defeating violence and that the means they employ is a form of love's knowledge.

Feelings and correct judgement: Tate Taylor's *The Help* (2011) and Jenji Kohan's *Weeds*, season 6, episode 3 (2010)

Nussbaum explains that feelings and correct judgement combine to form what she calls 'perceptive equilibrium' (Cohen, *Future* 73). The interpretive procedure here isolated involves the understanding that unfolds as one reads or views a story: 'bewilderment and hesitation may actually be marks of fine attention' (Cohen, *Future* 73). Nussbaum goes on to describe this process as 'an equilibrium in which concrete perceptions "hang beautifully together", both with one another and with the agent's general principles, an equilibrium that is always ready to reconstitute itself in response to the new' (Cohen, *Future* 73). Nussbaum is not eliminating moral duty and utilitarianism from ethics but suggesting that they need to be supplemented by or placed in equilibrium with perceptive feelings.

> This does not mean that the way of perceiving cannot make use of rules and universal principles … but it cannot use them and insist on leaving out [perceptive feelings] … The result of 'perceptive equilibrium' is that rules and universal principles are subject to refinement, even revision by the unfolding of the story: we must not fortify ourselves against the outcome, but be prepared to be bewildered, 'to wait and float and be actively passive' (Cohen, *Future* 74–5).

Feelings and correct judgement in The Help

The Help is a vivid example of the unfolding process of perceptive equilibrium. At first, Skeeter (Emma Stone), the main character, seems to be one of the group of upper-middle-class young white women of Jackson, Mississippi, in 1963, exceptional only in being unmarried. And her mother, like those of the other group members, most of whom are her childhood friends, thinks of little else but getting her married to an appropriate white male. As the film progresses, we see that Skeeter is different from her friends and even finally that her mother is different from the other mothers.

Skeeter's departure from her childhood friends – after graduating from high school, instead of marrying, like her friends, she goes off for four years to university – leads to her decision to write a book about the relationship between the 'coloured' help and their mistresses from the point of view of the help, particularly as she was raised by a black maid whom she loved and respected. Interviewing one of the maids, Skeeter discovers how unfairly and at times cruelly some of them are treated. Most noticeably, the hardship of being a maid becomes very apparent when she asks how it feels to raise someone else's child when your own must be raised by another.

This segregated culture maintains itself on the basis of rules and principles, particularly concerning the question of whether the 'coloured' help should be able to use the same toilet as white people. Hilly (Bryce Dallas Howard), one of Skeeter's closest friends, proposes mandatory legislation preventing the coloured help from using the toilets of whites because they carry 'different diseases' than Caucasians. Since Skeeter writes a column for the local newspaper, Hilly asks her to place this proposal in the paper. Skeeter hesitates but never expresses her uneasiness. Finally, when pushed by Hilly, she deliberately misprints a request concerning another charitable hobby horse of Hilly's, the collection of old coats; in place of the word 'coats', Skeeter places 'commodes', resulting in Hilly's front yard being full of toilets, with one recently potty-trained youngster showing off her new skills in one of them in front of all the neighbours.

Now we begin to see an equilibrium developing between the rules dividing black and white people and the feelings of the people involved. Hilly and her friends are wary of Skeeter, who does not overtly oppose her friends' complete acceptance of segregation but remains passively active. Indeed, she agrees to meet the man whom Hilly believes would be an ideal husband for her. The larger world beyond Jackson, Mississippi, is changing. Meanwhile, Medgar Evers, a black emancipator, and President Kennedy are both assassinated in the early 1960s, and even the maids realise that the old rules and principles are being called into question. When Hilly in uncontrollable and unjustifiable anger fires her maid, the response in the community is unexpected. This particular maid, Minny (Octavia Spencer), is known for being outspoken but is tolerated because she is the best cook in town. After being fired, she brings Hilly her favourite dessert, a chocolate pie. Watching her devour her second piece, Minny explains that the chocolate is her own excrement. For Hilly, this stunt constitutes a declaration of war, and she sets about victimising other maids whom she believes are sympathetic to Minny. Under attack, these maids agree to tell their stories to Skeeter.

A new problem now arises. If Skeeter publishes the stories of the maids, how will they be protected from retaliation from their white employers? Minny convinces Skeeter that even if she publishes the story of the chocolate pie, Hilly will never admit that the tale is about her. As the ringleader, Hilly will avoid public embarrassment by insisting that these stories are not about the people of Jackson, Mississippi. And, indeed, Hilly adopts that position in public, but she nonetheless plans to have her private revenge on Skeeter by exposing her to her mother. To her astonishment, Skeeter's mother, Charlotte (Allison Janney), does not disapprove of her daughter's recounting the chocolate-pie story. Instead, she stands up for Skeeter, suggesting that Hilly needs to clean her mouth, presumably not merely from the pie but in general. This turnaround is particularly significant since Skeeter's mother had fired their maid under public pressure from the Daughters of the American Revolution, an organisation that at that time promoted segregation. Now Charlotte brings rules and principles into perceptive equilibrium with feelings for her daughter. As she puts it to Skeeter, 'Someone has to be courageous in this family.' What becomes clear is that Charlotte harboured deep guilt about firing her maid whom everyone in the family, particularly Skeeter, adored. Now those feelings come into play when Skeeter suggests that they need to be reconsidered in view of Hilly's draconian application of the rules and principles of segregation to her maid Minny and to Skeeter.

Although a successful comedy, *The Help* has a serious point: to have a book containing an incident of a black maid feeding her excrement to her previous white employer in such a community is shocking and unprecedented, illustrating a new equilibrium, in Nussbaum's terms, between segregation rules and the principles and feelings of the victims of abusive bigotry. The film concludes, however, on a darker note. Hilly forces her friend Elizabeth to make a false accusation of stealing against her black maid, Aibileen (Viola Davis), a friend of Minny, Hilly's arch-enemy. In a heart-wrenching scene, Aibileen says goodbye to Elizabeth's child whom she has raised since birth and who is as attached to her as Skeeter was to Constantine. Aibileen, at first heartbroken, finally decides that she will retire and become a writer, turning her diaries into publishable material. She thus represents the notion that the struggle for equality for black people is by no means over. For, as Nussbaum makes clear, the ethics of perceptive equilibrium will always be a challenge to the status quo, in whatever form it takes in the future, and the courage of people like Skeeter and Aibileen in confronting bigotry will always be a part of the impulse towards a good or at least better life, the goal of ethics. *The Help* concludes by emphasising that the process may be long and arduous and that some people like Hilly may never see the light. In short, the idea of ethics, however worthy, may not be realisable in some contexts, for some people.

Feelings and correct judgement in Weeds, *season 6,*
episode 3
Although it begins in 2005, *Weeds* is the female equivalent of
the male series from three years later, *Breaking Bad*, analysed in
Chapter 4 above. Nancy Botwin (Mary-Louise Parker) is a single
mother with three children who sells marijuana and hashish to
keep her family afloat. This series is sustained by the brilliant and
versatile acting of Mary-Louise Parker who violates every rule and
principle of motherhood while convincing us that she is a caring
mother always doing what she believes is best for her children. It
is impossible in words to describe the subtle body language and
facial gestures that enable Nancy to communicate with her children.
Usually her response is a form of disapproval or impatience with
juvenile behaviour, but her unique skill is in making clear her disapproval in a form of tough love. Even when actually spanking Shane
(Alexander Gould), she intends only to emphasise the seriousness of
his infraction without hurting him.

Shane's infraction takes place during the opening scene of this
series that has been characterised, in understated terms, as a dark
comedy: overhearing a woman threatening the lives of Nancy's
children, Shane murders her. In the heated interchange between the
two women, Nancy had promised that if her children were harmed,
she would kill the woman. Shane follows his mother's principles,
even if that involves taking them more literally than she would have
wished. Clearly, Nussbaum's notion of an equilibrium between feelings and rules or principles is very apt. From this point on, Shane
and the Botwin family are fugitives from the law because Nancy
assumes that the family accepts Shane's need to flee from justice.
Indeed when Silas (Hunter Parrish), the oldest brother, objects that
the family decision to leave town involves his being punished for his
brother's crime, Nancy stops the car, making clear she understands
Silas's position, offering him the choice to leave and go his own way.
Like his mother, Silas decides to stay out of loyalty to the family.

Leaving town, the family hopes to evade the police and anyone
wishing to avenge the murder by changing their name and keeping
their heads low. The most fundamental question to consider in this
series is why an intelligent, attractive and able mother like Nancy
cannot find a decent job that provides a legally earned income and a
normal life for her family. This episode answers that question. Once
the family – Nancy's old boyfriend Andy (Justin Kirk) decides to

join them – have arrived in a town where they are not known, they attempt, under assumed names, to find jobs and live a normal life. Noticing a picket line in front of a hotel, they hope some openings are available to newcomers, but in spite of their smart appearance and clever interviews they are given the lowest positions, Andy as a dishwasher, Silas a bellhop, and Nancy a maid. Shane is to look after his baby brother while the others are at work. In short, the family now experiences the life of law-abiding citizens at the bottom of the working-world ladder. And here we shall find an answer to our question: what would happen to this family if they lived a normal life on the right side of the law?

Each soon comes to realise that living by the rules and principles prevents enjoyment of a normal life. Andy tries to offer his culinary skills to help the chef, who chokes him, telling him never to speak out of turn again. When Andy bakes a special cake to demonstrate his culinary skills, the chef puts his cigarette out in it. Silas, whose salary is mainly comprised of tips, discovers that his best tipper requires him to read while dressed only in his underwear. Nancy's experience is the most instructive. Entering a room to change the sheets, she finds a naked man chained to the bed nearly floating in urine-stained sheets. He explains that the hooker had to leave for her day job but left the keys to the lock. When she hesitates, he insults her, telling her not to judge him since she is just 'the fucking maid'. Quietly, Nancy sits down, pointing out that he is not in a position of power and should show more respect. His response is to offer her a $20 tip. She inquires if he has considered who would have to clean up this mess. Angrily, he retorts, 'It's your job.' Nancy smiles, lays down the clean linen, throws him the keys, exiting with the wonderful line, 'You can be your own maid, and don't worry about the tip', providing a rather bizarre example of equilibrium between the principle of doing what the job requires and the negative feelings that the employee can well justify about this particular job.

Later, downstairs, having a drink at the bar, Nancy is approached by a man who is clearly attracted to her. She seems to be doing well with this man, pretending to be a visitor to the hotel who has her own dance studio having just returned from Paris, the 'deuxième arrondissement'. Then her boss interrupts the conversation to tell her in front of the man that she is not allowed to drink at the hotel bar even when not on duty. Moreover, one of the best of their regular customers has called to complain that the maid refused to clean his room; she is peremptorily ordered to hurry upstairs to clean the room, where she is confronted with a note from the client with a tip, 'I love to pay people to clean up my mess.' The manager clearly enjoys berating Nancy in front of the male hotel guest not only because she has violated a rule of her position but also because he feels that in conversing at the bar she is getting above her proper place in the hotel hierarchy. This incident thus serves as a rather perverse form of ethical equilibrium between rules and feelings. So now she returns to the room reeking of urine where the social hierarchy says she belongs.

The point is that not only is the pay below what is essential for survival, but you are also treated like a slave, a whore, or both. As Nancy remarks to her family, she is less well paid than the whore who peed in the bed and has a dirtier job. The saddest moment is when Nancy, having been carpeted by her boss in front of a customer, is rendered speechless. In addition to underpaying the maid, her boss insists on destroying her self-respect. His position, no doubt also underpaid, seldom feels as powerful as when he is putting in their place those beneath him. The man upstairs in chains and urine-stained sheets can break the rules because he can afford what it takes to keep the manager quiet and happy; Nancy, by contrast, is less well paid and more rudely treated, we imagine, than his whore. The dilemma faced by Nancy and her three children, new to the bottom of the food chain, is that they are not only exploited monetarily but are also treated with indignity and disrespect, an unholy 'equilibrium' of rules, principles, and wounded feelings.

So Nancy does what she has done in the past: looks for an alternative that is not entirely legal but that is more likely to keep her family from more serious crime. She overhears the piano player telling Andy that the local weed salesman, one of the hotel employees, is refusing, while on strike, to sell weed. Adroitly, she locates the weed supplier, noticing that they are discarding parts of the plant they do not use. Gathering up this detritus, she uses the laundrette washing machines to cook these remains, which she then sells as hashish. At this point one may feel that the plot is so preposterous and comical that it is really not to be taken seriously. I would argue that the ethical issues are real and germane to our world, rendered comical and enjoyable to make them palatable. We can only judge Nancy to be an unfit mother if we use rules and principles as criteria. If feelings are added to the mix in equal proportion we are left in some doubt: are the rules and principles perhaps the refuge of those who exploit people in Nancy's position? And if we argue that the bosses also have little choice, then we have to consider the entire context that creates this situation. In any event, ethical perceptive equilibrium changes our perspective and suggests alternative resolutions.

Breaking Bad, the male equivalent of *Weeds*, shows Walter in a similar position, underpaid and undervalued, at least by everyone outside his immediate family. Both series go beyond the question of the individual ethics of the protagonists, Nancy and Walter, to indict a society that does not provide a means for decent working people to support their family, a social rather than personal ethical issue. In fact, as these two television series make clear, the doctrines of moral duty and of utilitarianism cannot in all fairness be applied: as Nussbaum argues, human feelings and a comprehension of the context must be considered if we are to establish ethical equilibrium.

Conclusion: the strands of the web of culture

This volume began with Clifford Geertz's image of culture as man 'suspended in webs of significance he himself has spun'. Understanding the significance of these webs requires thick description, a process characteristic of literary criticism. For this reason, Geertz concludes that anthropologists can profit from literary-critical methodology. As anthropologists adopt literary-critical ways, Geertz suggests that such a move affects both disciplines; in moving closer to the humanities, anthropologists influence literary criticism to make use of the methods of anthropology. And, in fact, in the last three decades of the twentieth century, that is precisely what happened. A number of literary commentators came to view themselves as cultural critics.

The reason some literary critics moved from culture in Matthew Arnold's sense of museums and libraries to culture with a broader meaning, ranging from banks and football stadiums to hospitals, that is, to what anthropologists call culture, resulted from linguistic analysis, particularly that of structuralism but also of other kinds of formalism. Although a special form of language, literature was seen as intimately bound up with language in general, one of the media of culture. For example, in T. S. Eliot's 'The Love Song of J. Alfred Prufrock', Prufrock speaks of the 'butt-ends of my days and ways', a metaphor suggesting that quotidian life passes like the smoking of a cigarette. In 1915, when the poem first appeared, smoking was a normal part of daily life. Now that it is no longer generally accepted many readers may be puzzled by this line or take it quite erroneously as relating only to the minority who continue to smoke. Our culture has radically changed its view of smoking, and the poetry of Eliot cannot escape that change: the word 'butt-ends' has a different meaning now than it did a century ago, and that difference is related less to museums and libraries than to banks and hospitals, particularly if we consider the cost of medical treatment for the physical ailments that result from smoking. Critical analysis of Eliot's poem must then engage in cultural criticism in order to make clear the nature of Prufrock's remark. Even the overall meaning of the 'The Love Song of J. Alfred Prufrock' is culturally bound; the narrative voice employs a technique known as *paysage intérieur*, interior landscape, which is designed to show how perception of the outward world is intimately bound up with and reveals the viewer's inner being, a technique that clearly derives from Freud and other psychoanalysts of the early twentieth century. Geertz's main contribution to literary theory is his insistence that analysis of culture is a form of textual exegesis, if text is taken in the broadest sense, ranging from books and newspapers to behavioural texts, dances, marches and wrestling matches. His concepts of the web of culture and thick description are key ideas throughout this study; from the point of view of literary theory, the two taken together imply that culture is a text/web whose significance is unlocked by thick description/literary-critical interpretation.

The above example from Eliot's poem is also historical in that it makes reference to a specific historical era, the early twentieth century. And here Hayden White, in Chapter 2, makes clear that the historian also crosses the border into the literary-critical realm. While Geertz emphasised interpretation to provide the anthropologist with depth or thickness of description, White focuses upon the fictive nature of literature that becomes important after the facts have been established and the historian incorporates them into a compelling narrative. Much of the connective tissue that binds the story together, gives it cohesion, cannot be documented, is often fictive in the sense that the historian imagines – a term dear to literary hearts – what would or could have happened under the circumstances. White thus furthers what Geertz calls the 'blurring' of genre boundaries, leading to the reconfiguring of genres. If history contains elements of fiction, then fiction often incorporates history in the form of actual events or imaginary occurrences that might have happened. The realistic novel, just one of the literary genres that could be cited, has frequently been defended in terms of probability. The new genre of 'faction' comes to mind. Blurring does not necessarily mean fusion. White is not arguing that novels are history or vice versa, only that historical novels are closer to history than, for example, fantasy or sci-fi. The point is that the distinction between literature and history remains even if it is now less clear-cut or more blurred than before. White's significant innovation is to apply Geertz's concept of interpretation to history and literature. The implication of this crossing of disciplinary borders is that the licence we give the historian to form a narrative and the 'suspension of disbelief' we allow the writer spinning a yarn are closely related, part of what might be called the psyche of the culture. The reader of historical narrative understands it as a story, responds to its cohesion and wholeness, by means of imaginative and fictive elements that derive from or are in our cultural psyche.

That psyche, however, is not wholly representative of the people of the culture, particularly of women, the oppressed, and the minorities. In Chapter 3, Julia Kristeva considered the question of how the female perspective can be fully integrated into the cultural psyche. She sees three stages as the means to this end, two that have already taken place and a third that remains an ideal, not beyond the bounds of possibility but yet to be accomplished. Having established certain rights that, although not yet fully realised, are generally recognised to be justifiable, such as, 'abortion, contraception, [and] equal pay', women gained entry into a world still dominated by male attitudes, rather like guests in someone else's, that is, men's homes. In response, women developed a language of their own, influenced by post-structuralist and post-formalist views of language as a cultural home. The final goal involves an end to hostilities between the sexes, where the inner beings of males and females, what Kristeva calls their nuclei, allow in and share equally with the other sex, leading not to the end of sexual difference but to an end to conflict between them. Presumably, the two languages will blend into one, forming a cultural home for both. With regard to literary criticism, it is not enough to tolerate the feminine or feminist perspective; that is to remain at phase two. The male and female critical perspectives must both be equally present in both male and female critics. Once again, the culture and cultural change are essential to the critical endeavour. Kristeva's contribution to cultural literary theory is to suggest that, if combined, the male and female perspective will enrich our culture by altering our critical perspective and our behaviour, based upon a female/male interpretive strategy. Moving beyond and consolidating the position of Geertz and White that interpretation is the basis of cultural critique, Kristeva asserts

that the interpretation must include the feminine perspective. Even
the male/female nucleus does not come to terms with the dilemma
of the minority perspective.

The position of the oppressed, the subaltern or the member of a
minority, presents a different problem, according to Homi K. Bhabha
in Chapter 4. Hybridity, the term Bhabha employs to describe the
oppressed and the oppressor, is a permanent scar derived from
exploitation that remains after oppression has ceased, if it ever does.
It is a psychic and cultural stain that must be confronted but is never
to be expunged unless history itself is erased. The record of the abuse
by people of people remains; the task, as Bhabha sees it, is to accept
and understand this position and cease to think oppressed people
can be appeased or mollified. If that sounds very negative, there is a
positive side. The culture that accommodates this position broadens
the critical perspective; instead of regret and futile attempts at apology, hybridity, for Bhabha, should be welcomed into the mind-set
of the critic, opening up new vistas of interpretation and offering a
place for its unique perspective in interpretive discourse. Although
the right of physical equality for the subaltern has been accepted,
it is now time to offer the same to the mentality of hybridity. Once
again, the boundaries of the cultural psyche are being blurred. The
paradox for Bhabha is that only when the master offers the subaltern's hybridity full intellectual legitimacy will they recognise their
own hybridity, since the one does not exist without the other. Which
I suppose is one way of saying you can only as an intellectual forgive yourself when you accept or forgive the intellect of the other.
South Africa comes to mind, but what culture is without similar
problems of racism and other forms of bigotry? Bhabha's contribution to cultural literary theory is to suggest how the inclusion of
hybridity within the critical perspective is necessary for both the
oppressed and the oppressor: again, the assumption, shared by all
the theorists in this volume, is that the cultural dilemma we all face
requires interpretation. For Bhabha, interpretation must include the
perspective of the oppressed/oppressor.

For both Kristeva and Bhabha, culture has become a larger, more
collective phenomenon: the changes they envisage are on a broad
scale involving not only the intellectuals but the whole population, since altering the intellectual mind-set will eventually change
the entire society. Sociology, the study of society as a whole, thus
becomes the next subject, in Chapter 5 on Pierre Bourdieu. The

constrictions and boundaries of change in society are analysed by
Bourdieu, who very adroitly uses sociological methodology but
avoids the determinism of laws and rules; he, too, is an advocate
of thick description, the methods of literary interpretation. He
finds that the ultimate limitations of a culture nonetheless allow
for important individual differences, but the limitations need to be
clearly understood. They are, as we would expect, both inner and
outer. Habitus, Bourdieu's term for the inner boundaries, is placed
in contexts or fields. The outer boundaries for Bourdieu are not
merely passive settings but locations of great stress and competition
where a habitus is put under pressure and tested because others are
vying for the desirable positions in any field. And, most importantly,
the interaction of a habitus in a field involves not only a mental
attitude and capacity but also behaviour, physical action. The result
of this interaction of a habitus in a field leads to a lifestyle. The
social limitations are ultimate but offer sufficient manoeuvrability
within for difference of character. In literary terms, the context does
not completely determine the character. Nevertheless, these outer
boundaries are the determinants of culture in a collective sense. If
we return to Geertz's image of the web of culture, Spider-Man, for
Bourdieu, is a choice of lifestyle that appears to have perfect freedom, permitting flight above the people below immobilised by traffic jams. Bourdieu reminds us that the skyscrapers form the outer
limits of his flight and establish the boundaries of his web. The culture of New York City represented by those tall buildings is something that even Spider-Man cannot transcend; in fact he confronts it
when in the air as much as when he is on the ground with the rest
of us. Bourdieu's contribution to literary theory is in establishing
the outer limits of culture, limits that nonetheless permit individual
differences. He insists that no analysis of the individual in context
is complete without an interpretive understanding of the limitations
of the culture.

If, as Bourdieu insists, culture provides ultimate limitations,
boundaries that are impassable, what happens when there is an
ethical conflict between cultures, as when 'honour killings' occur
in Western countries? Martha Nussbaum, in Chapter 6, confronts
this kind of problem. Nussbaum argues for an ethics based on
literary-critical principles as an alternative to Kant's moral duty and
Bentham's utilitarianism. Love's knowledge, for Nussbaum, involves
beginning not with the rule or regulation of right and wrong or with

what promotes a useful end but with empathy for the individual and a grasp of their situation, precisely what the critic describes as a close reading of a text. Moreover, judgement of the individual must first analyse the action and thought from the point of view of that individual rather than what a utilitarian or Kantian would consider the preferred choice. In literary-critical terms, Nussbaum is arguing for what is called the *donnée* of the text: a provisional granting on the part of the reader of the context or situation of the text and, as in the novel when characters are involved, of the habitus of the character. Nussbaum's ethics becomes from the perspective of the critic an act of critical reading. Abstract absolutes of duty and utility are waved aside as too thin, in Geertz's terms. The specific person and the concrete context must be examined in detail and evaluated. So where does that leave us with regard to the honour killings? A thick cultural description shows us that the problem is not necessarily murder motivated by personal animus. Rather, this crime is deeply cultural, and the perpetrators are almost always members of the victim's family, mainly fathers, uncles, and brothers. Now living in the West, these people have access presumably to social institutions designed, at least in principle, to replace the neighbourhood guardian or honour killer. Here, I believe, tolerance of another culture stops. Indeed, in her essay of 1989, Nussbaum expresses some disappointment that ethics of the sort she promulgates is not of more interest to literary critics. Perhaps the answer is that ethics cannot always accept the boundaries of culture. Nussbaum's contribution to cultural critique is to suggest that interpretation – which for her as for all the others in this volume involves thick description – must move beyond any single culture, including ethical values that reside at a higher level than that of culture itself. Although ethical thick description is a cultural as well as textual or specific endeavour, ethics may cause great problems in attempts to cross cultural boundaries. In this respect, Nussbaum's ethics may have prepared the way for the move beyond culture theory.

Present-day disillusionment with cultural critique can be seen in a recent volume of *New Literary History* (45.3, summer 2015), entitled 'Beyond Bourdieu and Other Essays'. One of the commentators in this volume, Bernard Lahire, points out that Bourdieu's analysis of art leads to meaning in art being reduced to the 'literary field'. Works of art 'in form as well as content – are viewed as wholly explicable through the authors' positions in the field'. The result is that a writer is reduced to 'a strategist who is only reacting to past or present rivals'. Lahire continues, 'Bourdieu often reduces an individual's life path to a trajectory conceived as a series of 'positions' occupied in a structured space' (389). Clearly the complaint here against Bourdieu is reminiscent of Nussbaum's difficulties with Kant and Bentham. The approach is too thin and abstract, leaving out all elements of individuality, and the specific text or work of art is subsumed in a field of competition taking precedence over personal expression. As Nussbaum demonstrates, ethics without the concrete context and the specific individual is not ethics or at least not ethical. The affair between culture critique and literary criticism seems to have ended. That is the subject of another book, my next project. Here it is sufficient to note that the cultural moment for literary theory has led to the integration of elements, disciplines, and positions previously excluded from the programme: anthropological stories (Geertz), the historical use of fiction (White), feminism within not merely tolerated without (Kristeva), post-colonialism as a valid perspective (Bhabha), sociological analysis of collective culture (Bourdieu), and ethics as an element of culture (Nussbaum). Finally, ethics seems to be at the heart of the break with Bourdieu, who is seen now as overly deterministic, a social scientist whose theories do not fully accommodate individuals, from Geertz's thick description to Nussbaum's love's knowledge. The very fact that cultural theory has been deconstructed by two of its most important ideas is testament to its importance as a historical moment in the continuum of theory and, more importantly, one that sheds light on the main dilemma of our time: the clash of cultures. With all of its assets and limitations, advantages and disadvantages, we cannot avoid consideration of culture in all its manifestations, from art to parking spaces, from architectural achievements to medical services, from all created objects to all resident subjects.

Since assessment and analysis of cultures has become so important and prevalent, what better source for studying it than film and television? Of all the artistic media, it is far and away the broadest in scope, communicating with an audience that is larger and more varied than any other art form. Although it can be argued that certain technological elements, the smart phone or the web, reach a larger audience, film and television, unlike these complex mechanical objects, are interpretive media, not merely a means of communication but a goal-directed activity. Films and television have a message, while someone has to use a phone or the web to send or receive a message. And although Marshall McLuhan informed us some time ago that the medium is the message, that message has been received: unless we learn how to interpret it, we shall hear little more than white noise.

The interpretation that I bring to film and television is that of a non-specialist seeking a means of demonstrating how the arcane and erudite ideas of literary theory are seeping into the general culture, not because these two media have a special relationship; on the contrary, they seem as far apart as ever. Rather, the ideas of cultural literary theory form the basis for our ways of coping with daily life. *Spider-Man 2* is a film about how our young people need a hero, as the subway riders tell Peter Parker, to cope with life in the Big Apple. The web spun by Spider-Man helped me explain Geertz's concept of culture, but since the dimensions of the skyscrapers limit the web to which it is attached, it also served as an instance of Bourdieu's concept of the outer limits of culture. My point is that the films and television programmes have a life of their own; they pursue their own purposes, that is, of the director/producer, and only incidentally are useful to illustrate my analysis of any theorist. At the end of each of my analyses of the films and television programmes I have tried to indicate how they differ from or proceed in a different direction from that of the theory being discussed. It should also be kept in mind that almost any of the films and television selections could be used to exemplify other theories than those I have chosen.

The fact that movies and television are independent works of art with their own goals also serves my purpose, for they thereby suggest that the ideas contained in them are arrived at independently, demonstrating the general presence in the culture of these ideas. For example, the *House of Cards* episode used to illustrate White's notion of how fiction and fact join to make history could also relate to Kristeva's point about the war of the sexes. Viewing Frank and Claire as modern Macbeth and Lady Macbeth helps explain how Claire advances the position of women to being nearly equal to that of men, that is, to the position of vice-president. In a strangely perverse way, Claire comes to represent Kristeva's second phase of feminism, incorporating in her being every bit of the ruthless ambition of her husband and a willingness equal to that of any man to use force to maintain her position. The fact that *House of Cards* is not limited by White's or Kristeva's notions but pursues its own end makes evident that the concepts, like White's of the mingling of fact and fiction in history or Kristeva's of the stages towards a male/female psyche, are at large in the culture.

It may be objected, however, that the films do not contain these ideas but are uncovered or discovered by my interpretation, my attempt at thick description. Admittedly, these ideas are a function of my goal of making theory clear to non-specialists: not immanent in the films, the ideas are the result of my interpretive project. The quest for interpretation is itself embedded in our culture, of which my book is but a manifestation. For example, Iron Man is an inveterate interpreter, and the films featuring him have been highly successful in reaching an audience that ranges from adolescents to their parents and grandparents, if I am at all representative. Iron Man proclaims at the beginning of *Iron Man 2* that he has successfully 'privatised' the armaments market with a weapon of weapons that cannot be duplicated: his interpretation of this phenomenon is that world peace can thus be guaranteed. When it becomes clear that Ivan Vanko has a weapon nearly as lethal as his, Iron Man revises his interpretation; in *Iron Man 3* he asserts that we make our own demons, that is, since Vanko could only acquire the resources for his weapon from the United States, the real enemy is not Vanko but an American supplier. Iron Man's final interpretation is that war cannot be ended with technology alone; people must decide what they are willing to sacrifice for peace, so Iron Man, in a gesture of love for Pepper and with the goal of ending war, destroys the Iron Man suits of armour. *Iron Man 3* thus suggests that interpretation is necessary to find a resolution to the clash of cultures. The need for a thick or deeper understanding of this dilemma is apparent as millions of immigrants wait at the gates of western Europe on a scale not seen since the mass emigrations of the Second World War.

In fact, the need to analyse culture clash, from within and without, is prevalent in every chapter of this study. *Iron Man*, of Chapter 1, as was suggested earlier, focused on this problem. *The Butler*, in Chapter 2, contrasts the worlds of black and white people in the United States; the struggle between Cecil the butler and his eldest son as to whether violence or non-violence is the best way to achieve equality involves interpretation. While Cecil finds that polite persistence is not enough, his son discovers that he is unwilling to kill for the cause. Father and son finally come together at a rally against South African Apartheid policy that is more overt than Cecil's previous endeavours and less violent than his son's past attempts. They have both come to understand that they need to push but not shove, a behavioural text or interpretation: equality is forwarded by awakening the consciences of the members of the establishment without getting their backs up.

In Chapter 3, the cultural conflict of *Spanglish* involved the Latino versus the Anglo-Saxon community. Flor believes that she needs to decide how much to encourage her daughter Cristina to integrate into the majority culture of the United States. Deciding not to permit Cristina to take up the scholarship at the exclusive private school in the upper-middle-class suburb, Flor insists that Cristina stay in touch with her Mexican immigrant roots. At first, Cristina is heartbroken, but, upon growing older, she revises her interpretation of her mother's decision. Now, applying for university admission, she realises that her mother has not deprived her of the best education but has given her an opportunity for a unique kind of knowledge; she has learned to straddle two cultures, that of her origins in Mexico and that of her new home in the United States. Her uniqueness in that respect might just be what will put her ahead of the others applying to Princeton, but, more importantly, it makes a virtue of an inconvenience: the need to emigrate from Mexico to the United States, however difficult and disruptive, has resulted in her acquiring a perspective that includes both cultures, the fruit of her mother's interpretation.

In Chapter 4, the culture clash in *Breaking Bad* is between the rich and the poor of the United States. Struggling to support his family as a chemistry teacher, Walter turns to drugs in order to take his family out of working poverty. Diagnosed with a fatal form of cancer, he decides to shoulder responsibility for criminality and leave the rewards of his illegal endeavours for his family to inherit. Walter's interpretation is that the stigma of criminality is less debilitating – and he should know since his son is handicapped – than struggling to live on minimum-wage or less-than-minimum-wage jobs. His analysis, of course, involves an indictment of his culture: that one of the wealthiest countries in the world cannot provide its 'honest' workers with a better career opportunity than criminality. The controversial nature of this indictment is itself an indication that it is an interpretation, and very likely not one shared by all.

Having already discussed *House of Cards* from Chapter 5, I move on to Chapter 6. *Peaky Blinders* concerns class conflict in

1920s England. And, as in *Breaking Bad*, the choice for the lower class is between political activism, represented by Freddie, the communist, and the criminality of the gang led by Tommy. The conversation in the pub between these two men, friends during the war but now rivals, is important: Tommy points out to Freddie that they both offer false hope to the poor but that his bookie business occasionally pays off. The implication is that Freddie is up against an establishment, represented by the Tory minister Winston Churchill, that will not help the poor, considering communism as criminal as the actions of the Peaky Blinders. However inaccurate and grim, Tommy's lifestyle is based upon an interpretation of the political state at the time.

Interpretation of culture clash is at present a characteristic of our society. For that reason, this phase of literary theory is of particular pertinence at this time. Why theory? Because cultural theory and the need to understand and interpret it is embedded in our culture – alive and well in movies and television.

Bibliography

Bhabha, Homi K. *The Location of Culture*. London and New York: Routledge, 1994.

Bourdieu, Pierre. *Distinction: A Social Critique of the Judgement of Taste*. Trans. Richard Nice. London and New York: Routledge, 1984.

Cohen, Ralph, Ed. *The Future of Literary Theory*. London and New York: Routledge: 1989.

——. 'Literary Theory as a Genre'. *Centrum*. (Spring 1975): 45–65.

Croce, Benedetto. *History as the Story of Liberty*. New York: ACLS, 2009. First published 1938.

Dickens, Charles. *Great Expectations*. Ed. Edgar Rosenberg. New York: W. W. Norton, 1999. First published 1861.

——. *A Tale of Two Cities*. Stockholm: Wisehouse Classics, 2016. First published 1859.

Frye, Northrop. *Anatomy of Criticism*. Princeton, NJ: Princeton University Press, 1957.

Geertz, Clifford. *Local Knowledge: Further Essays in Interpretative Anthropology*. London: Fontana Press, 1993.

Kristeva, Julia. *The Kristeva Reader*. Ed. Toril Moi. New York: Columbia University Press, 1986.

Litch, Mary M. and Amy Karofsky. *Philosophy through Film*. London and New York: Routledge, 2002.

Melas, Natalie. *All the Difference in the World: Postcoloniality and the Ends of Comparison*. Palo Alto, Calif.: Stanford University Press, 2007.

New Literary History. 43.3 (spring 2015).

Nussbaum, Martha C. *Love's Knowledge*. Oxford: Oxford University Press, 1990.

Richter, David H. *The Critical Tradition: Classic Texts and Contemporary Trends*, 3rd edn. Boston, Mass., and New York: Bedford and St. Martin's Press, 2007.

Tomarken, Edward L. *Filmspeak: How to Understand Literary Theory by Watching Movies*. New York: Bloomsbury Academic, 2012.

Wellek, René and Austin Warren. *Theory of Literature*. New York: Harcourt Brace, 1949.

Index